What a Coincidence!

What a Coincidence!

the *wow!* factor in synchronicity
and what it means in everyday life

Susan M. Watkins

Moment Point Press
Needham, Massachusetts

Moment Point Press, Inc.
PO Box 920287
Needham, MA 02492
www.momentpoint.com

Cover design: Susan Ray and Metaglyph Design
Typesetting: A & B Typesetters & Publishing Services
Printing: McNaughton & Gunn
Distribution: Red Wheel / Weiser

Library of Congress Cataloging-in-Publication Data

Watkins, Susan M., 1945–
What a coincidence! : the wow! factor in synchronicity
and what it means in everyday life / Susan M. Watkins—1st ed.
p. cm.
Includes bibliographical references.
ISBN-13: 987-1-930491-07-6 (pbk. : alk. paper)
ISBN-10: 1-930491-07-7 (pbk. : alk. paper)
1. Coincidence. I. Title.
BF1175.W38 2005
130—dc22
2005012273

Printed in the United States on recycled acid-free paper
10 9 8 7 6 5 4 3 2 1

In memory of Evelyn Cizek Storch,
lost comrade in all things mysterious.

Also by Susan M. Watkins

Conversations with Seth, books 1 & 2
Speaking of Jane Roberts
Garden Madness
Dreaming Myself, Dreaming a Town

Contents

1

Yikes! What Was That?

A *Few* Opening Salvos

1. I'm standing by the register in the local organic foods store in Watkins Glen, New York, talking with co-owner Bob about the upcoming Thanksgiving holiday as he bags my purchases. He says that he and his wife are going to stay home and take a much-needed day of rest. I tell him I'm going to stay home myself, and watch a couple Woody Allen movies. Bob says, that's funny—he's been thinking all day about his favorite Woody Allen movies, especially "Sleeper." Laughing gently at himself, he says, you remember "Sleeper," don't you—where the guy wakes up in the next century and the health foods are sugar and cigarettes?

Instantly, as if on precise cue, as Bob says the word "cigarettes," the door opens and a girl sticks her head in the store and asks, "Have you got cigarettes?"

Bob gapes at her, can barely stammer out the word, "No." The girl scowls, goes away. The irony is so pointed that Bob and I just stare at one another, speechless. This is, after all, an organic foods store, clearly marked, unmistakable for what it is, the antithesis of the "Sleeper" setting—exactly what director Woody Allen had in mind as an object of satire. Like a spontaneous dovetailing of ideas or a direct comment, conjured up by—what? Our conversation? A universe with a sense of humor? Mere chance, nothing more?

2. I see an ad on television for the VHS-DVD issue of Robert DeNiro's movie "Ronin." As when it first came out, the movie's title is a mystery to me and I wonder what it means, but for some reason I don't bother to look it up in the dictionary. Then later that same evening, I'm reading Kim Stanley Robinson's alternate history epic *The Years of Rice and Salt*,[1] and lo there's a speech by a Japanese sailor who describes himself as "a ronin, a warrior without a tribe." Hey, thank you Kim Stanley!

Fast-forward a year and a half: I'm reading through my notes to put this book together, combing for examples of how coincidences from the past often connect with the present in a strange wormhole-like manner, and I come across this quirky little business with the word "ronin." It's not one of those past-present connections, but it's neat anyway and so I decide to include it in a list format I have in mind for the opening chapter. So later that same evening, I'm surfing through the TV channels at a friend's house and there's "Ronin" scheduled on the movie package my friend just happens to subscribe to. It's such a little coincidence, really, that most people probably wouldn't spend a millisecond thinking about it, but then I turn to CNN and there's a news report about a huge car crash in Fresno, California—and how funny that this morning, the same morning I came across my old notes about the "ronin" thing, I had also read notes I'd written up two years ago about a chain of coincidences involving a big car crash in Fresno, California!

What just happened here? Did I invoke something? Did these events rise up out of the past, come back to life somehow, in response to my focus on them? Or am I just noticing patterns that mean nothing outside of the fact that I'm inclined to notice patterns?

3. My friend Kay tells me this story: Her teenaged daughter has been staying overnight several times a week at a girlfriend's house in a nearby hamlet, where that family had recently moved. For some reason, Kay starts having recurring nightmares that this friend's house catches fire and burns to the ground while her daughter is in it. These dreams (understandably) distress Kay so much that whenever her daughter is at the friend's house, Kay sets her alarm for 2 or 3 A.M., dials the family's phone number and lets it ring until somebody answers and Kay hangs up. "You know, so if there's a fire, they'd see it," she tells me. "I don't do things like that, but those dreams are too real! I even see the front of the house fall over in flames! Do you blame me for making those calls?"

Well, *I* certainly don't. Two weeks after Kay confesses this little transgression of manners to me, her daughter is staying overnight at the girlfriend's place and the house *next door* burns to the ground! No one was home, and no one was injured in the fire, which was discovered by a passing motorist at 12:30 A.M. And according to news reports, the front of the house did indeed fall over, engulfed in flames, exactly as Kay had seen it happen, night after night, in her dreams.

So what does this mean? That Kay saw what was going to happen because the fire might endanger her daughter, sleeping next door? Did her protective instincts prowl into the near future and send back a warning, though slightly off-target, of trouble to come? Or is this just a coincidence, meaning nothing in itself, since mothers everywhere worry about their children even when, as is usually the case, no bad things happen to them?

4. I'm looking over my checkbook and come to the rueful conclusion that I'm going to be a tad short of money this month. Obviously, I need to do something about this, but instead of going out and looking for a job like a normal person, I pretend that money comes to me in some unforeseen way. I do this by imagining myself walking down to my mailbox, opening up the mailbox, pulling out an envelope, opening the

envelope—all this in as much detail as I can muster—and finding therein a check for an amount that covers my temporary deficit. I run through this imaginary scenario once or twice, and then, typical of me, I get involved with something else and the whole unpleasant matter slides right out of my head.

Next morning I walk down to the mailbox, open it up, and pull out an envelope with a return address from a small online bookstore that carries hardcover copies of my book, *Dreaming Myself, Dreaming a Town*, by now at least five years out of print. Inside the envelope is a check for an amount that very nicely and then some covers my "temporary deficit," as I'd so optimistically described it to myself. How about that! I hadn't heard anything from this bookstore in a long time and I'd consciously forgotten the deal with my book; we have no formal royalty payment schedule, no semi-annual reports, nothing like that at all. The check just—arrived. By chance? By ESP? This isn't the first time I've noticed that coincidence and precognition are often intertwined. On the other hand, maybe my unconscious keeps better track of book sales than I do. Or had my imagination influenced this somehow? Had I nudged myself into an event (the earned royalties, the check's precise timing) that from yesterday's perspective had been one of infinite possibilities in a wide-open universe?

Of course there are millions of people out there imagining like crazy that they'll win the lottery whenever they spend that proverbial dollar. So why doesn't it work every time? If anything "works" at all, in those terms. Are the hits just numerical probabilities, meaningless in themselves? Or is there something else going on here, some combination of these explanations that simply hasn't occurred to us to consider?

5. My childhood best friend Evelyn calls me up one evening in late July. We've lived fifty-some miles apart for most of our adult lives and haven't seen or talked with one another in a while, but as always there's a strong, almost mystical connection between us. As we gab, it becomes

clear to me that Evelyn is in the throes of some serious emotional troubles. She is what you might call fixated on the idea of talking everyone she knows into moving to Myrtle Beach, the oceanside resort in South Carolina, where she's decided she wants to relocate with all her friends and relatives. "We'd all be together where it's warm," she says. "None of us would ever be alone." In the course of our conversation, she mentions this Myrtle Beach idyll probably half a dozen times.

Mixed with this, we also talk about the summers she and I spent as teenagers with my parents on Keuka Lake, in New York's Finger Lakes region, a setting we used to fantasize as the perfect afterlife, if there was one to be had, with various choice friends included—similar to Evelyn's current dream, actually, though I don't say this (our old fantasy comes to my mind as she talks). Now a mere fifteen-minute drive from my house, Keuka seems more distant than it was all those years ago, when it took a couple hours to get there in our overloaded station wagon, Ev and me riding in the back with our feet hanging out the window, laughing at everything, carefree as the wind. Thus I certainly know how it feels to long for something unattainable, as Evelyn's Myrtle Beach so plainly exemplifies. There's nothing I can do for her but listen, and commiserate. We talk for hours.

Next morning I relate this conversation to my friend Dave, who then suggests in his own commiserly way that we take his boat over to one of the state parks on Keuka Lake and go out for a sightsee—would I like that? I sure would, and we arrive there early enough so there's hardly any activity on the lake and nobody at the launch site at all, most unusual for summer. As we're getting the boat ready to put in the water, I notice a large colorful towel that somebody's left behind on the pier. It looks fairly new and clean, so I pick it up. On it is a lush tropical scene with the words MYRTLE BEACH in big, happy letters!

The impact this has on me in the moment, as I stand there staring at the towel, is almost impossible to describe. It's as if Evelyn's yearning has emerged into the scenery around me—the exact lake scenery she and I had discussed just the day before in specific regard to her Myrtle Beach dreams—to connect with me and tell me—what? Is there a message here, carried up from the depths in some ebb and flow of circumstance and timing, sent from her to me? Something engineered by the two of us; something that knew exactly where I'd be this morning, even though coming over here for a boat ride was spur-of-the-moment, the only conscious thought-progression from Ev's phone call to this place rising out of parallel efforts to console?

But that's ridiculous! It's just somebody's lost towel! You read Dear Abby letters all the time about people finding pennies with meaningful dates on them, and every time you think, Oh, come on. Talk about the "stupid power of personal involvement," as statisticians would say. Meaningless!

I kept the towel. As it turned out, its significance would accumulate, as a kind of harbinger of unconscious knowledge. Three years later, when Evelyn's husband called to tell me that she had died unexpectedly,[2] I realized with sudden vivid clarity that I'd been looking at the Elmira paper's obituary page first thing every morning for months, expecting to see her name.

6. It's mid-June, 2004. I've sold my house and am mogging around in my new apartment, fussing with furniture arrangements, when for some reason, no obvious outward connection to anything, I start thinking about the day three or four years ago when I ran into a woman I'll call Lonnie at the county recycling center.

I had known Lonnie back in the seventies, when we'd both lived near Dundee, but hadn't seen her in at least twenty years, until that day at the recycling center, sometime in the early summer of 2000 or 2001. For no reason apparent to me, I remember the scene clearly: I was putting plastic jugs in a bin when a woman walked up to me and said, "Why, hello, Sue!" in a friendly tone—and I didn't know who she was at all. Could not place her. Not a clue. I just stood there and stared at her, caught completely off guard. Finally, she identified herself as Lonnie, and I was mortified at not recognizing her, though I don't know why I should have been, as we were mere acquaintances of occasional happenstance chat, separated by years and circumstance.

So here in 2004, I further recall that Lonnie and I had a pleasant conversation that day beside the plastics bin. She seemed genuinely interested in what I was up to, and asked about my writing. I hadn't seen Lonnie since then. Coming out of my reverie about it, I wonder what she's been up to herself these days.

Next afternoon, I walk downtown to the local pizza shop and order a take-out salad for dinner. As I'm waiting for it at the counter, someone's voice from behind me says, "Why, hello, Sue!" I turn around and see a woman standing there wearing a flowery top and tan pants. I don't recognize her at all. I have no idea who she is. Not a clue! But she's smiling in a friendly way, expecting a reply, and here I am caught flat-footed, how embarrassing. Then I notice she's wearing a name tag on her bodice— and it's none other than Lonnie!

I'm momentarily stupefied by this—by this what? Connection of thought, time, place, words? Then it flashes through my mind that this completely unexpected greeting situation is an almost exact duplicate of the one at the recycling center: her recognizing me right off, versus me not recognizing her at all. I manage to collect my thoughts enough to ask what she's up to these days and she explains she's a home health aide, lives in another county now, and commutes between various far-flung jobs. Then she pays for her pizza and rushes out with a hasty bye-bye, and that's that.

I'm left with a very strange feeling, as if I'd accidentally come out in public wearing my pajamas. It isn't just that I had been thinking about her the day before running into her; I'd been thinking about the specific elements of our interaction (she: hello; me: huh?), and though logically you'd think my recollection should have helped me today, the exact setup of my not recognizing her had reoccurred. This is only the second time I've come in this particular restaurant and I can't remember if I'd planned on doing so yesterday, when the memory of Lonnie and me at the plastics bin had come into my head so vividly. I don't think so, but even if it had, it hardly makes a difference in the numberless factors that had to mesh for us to meet today, and in the particular choreography that mirrors our previous encounter so well.

A lesson in the efficacy of random thought? A remark from the universe on the subject of my people skills? Just a chance encounter attached to one of an infinite number of thoughts about anything I might have in a day? Except that this coincidence (as with all the others excerpted here from my records) carries a sensation of import with it, even if I can't exactly grasp what that import might be.

That's the thing about coincidence that is so intriguing, and not a little infuriating: it always seems to be *about* something, though what that something might be is often fleeting, whisked by in a blink of the inner eye. Moreover, coincidental events tend to act in smooth concert with precognition and an odd sort of clairvoyance, in which one's imagination (or imagined scenarios) is at the center of the coincidence cluster. Or, even more fascinating, the clusters can involve life elements that you're not consciously aware of at all. Some of these clusters are small and insignificant-seeming, of nothing more than momentary notice; others evolve into such complex mega-mindtwisters of association and connection that they veer off into the infinite, if not the absurd.

Of course the conscious mind is always engaged in sorting through the complex clues and nonverbal data of everyday life, chugging along behind our physical perceptions. We see what we're looking at, and organize the data to make sense of things in a world that we choose to experience in linear fashion. Experience may not, in fact, be linear at all, but that is how we believe our senses operate, in a loose sort of agreement that makes our social systems possible (if not always successful), not to mention our personal daily reality. And yet, coincidence, like dreams (and possibly the only difference between the two is that one appears in the waking state; more on that later), doesn't operate in a vacuum. The connections are always personal, even on the largest mass-event scale (again, more on that later), and almost always reflect what you think is possible to begin with . . . or they jar your idea of the possible with a certain disconcertingly gleeful irony. So who's making the joke?

Well, what if the mind is sorting through far more than what we think of as daily life, and has literally an infinite reach, encompassing everything that is possible and probable in a constant, dazzling organizational display from which we pick and choose the shape of our experience? What if the workings of that display show itself all the time, in a "paranormal" context that we tend to ignore or belittle? What if everything we need to know is contained in our conscious minds, of which we habitually employ the merest surface layer? How could we consciously employ these different forms of information, and what would it mean to us in the daily practical world to do so? And how far should we go with this idea? After all, some of history's worst acts of inhumanity have claimed justification in mystical realms. To our credit, so have the arts, as well as leaps of faith and courage that work to right the wrongs. Thus we gain nothing by denying the inherent possibilities of consciousness. Proving what these might be is another story. Using common sense about it is the central challenge.

Actually, I'm not sure that anyone, certainly including myself, can ever come to an empirical conclusion about coincidence, precognition, and clairvoyance; or that a "conclusion" in that sense is even possible. There are a number of books and studies of coincidence out there, and almost all of them fall into the expected opposing camps: Either we're fooling ourselves by believing there's hidden meaning in an objective universe, or coincidences are messages from the deity, giving us an elbow in the ribs when we need it most. Neither gives much credence to the central figure—the individual.

The problem is, a lot of nonsense has been attached to the entire subject of alternate perception, ESP, dreams, precognition, and the like, not to mention the debilitating culture wars that tend to spring up around nonsense in general. But to take the stance that such things as dreams and coincidence are meaningless seems to me a hopeless folly, cutting one's self off as it does from an entire psychological landscape in a way that can only diminish our sense of community and optimism. This division between the measurement of things by what we think of as objectivity or by the aegis of mysticism is, in its extremes, and especially when we become convinced that they're the same thing and our group has the correct interpretation, at the heart of our most appalling human troubles. On the other hand, just stating the polemic that "the mind and body are one" doesn't mean much, either.

Thus for me the idea that coincidence is merely a misunderstood statistic (though it can be exactly that) or the function of a brain that evolved to recognize patterns in a world filled with lethal randomness certainly isn't incorrect; it's more what I'd call the top layer of the picture. We create the events; we create the instruments to measure the events. The measurements are trustworthy, pragmatic, often beautiful. They show us the fantastic intricacy of our world. They lead us out of abject superstition toward science, scholarship, technology; and depending on them for everything, we've managed to mess things up but good. On the other hand, the messes we've made on behalf of the divine are much older and arguably more catastrophic. Moreover as witness current events, divine convictions are now armed with technology. Some nudge!

Somewhere in the middle lies a window to the workings of consciousness; clues as to how and why we got here and maybe even a way to mitigate (or at least expose the roots of) the messes. And this is where I think an anecdotal, yet sensible look-see at coincidence and oddball connections and encounters is worth a study, or at least an inquiry, without specifying proof or disproof as an absolute (though surely we will keep our wits about us). For this adventure, I'll be drawing almost completely on my own records, which I've kept for nearly thirty-seven years on an almost daily basis. Along with my dreams, I write down my observations of coincidence, precognition, and similar experiences; and in those thirty-seven years I've documented literally thousands of such occurrences. Backing these up are attached materials in the form of news clips, magazine articles, photographs, postcards, letters, email, and the occasional odd object (a found handkerchief; delicate hummingbird feathers; the door off an old toy car), as well as updated annotations and analysis that I add as the years go by.

Out of all this I've extracted coincidence examples that are not too personal, and are indicative of the point I hope to make: that these clusters, like dreams, create stories that enlarge upon reality, and it is in these stories—my stories here for the most part, but in your stories too—that the nature of our psyche reveals itself, with an inherent balance and precision native to us all. As Sam Harris puts it in *The End of Faith*,[3] such inquiries into the nature of consciousness, like other forms of knowledge, can be explored rationally, with the tools of reason, without recourse to credulity. And, I would add, while remaining comfortably ensconced in the spacious present, a more fulsome arena than we might suppose.

So let us follow some of these (always astonishing and sometimes extremely complex) coincidental trails and examine how they weave in and out of the forest of experience, and see what they might reveal, in all their intricate and surprising forms of encounter.

2

Conjuring the Eleemosynary
Prediction, Coincidence, and
the Contents of the Mind

During my senior year in high school, my group of hang-out buddies and I made up a game we called "new word of the week." This was back in the dark ages before computers, satellite TV, cell phones, or shopping malls (though we did have unlimited access to cards and bowling), so bear with me here on the subject of simple-minded pleasures in days of yore. We'd romp into English class first thing every school morning and grab the big old unabridged dictionary off the bookshelf, floof the pages, all eyes closed, jostling and galumphing like a bunch of pasture colts, until one of us stabbed a finger down on a definition; and that would be our word, which we would then proceed to repeat over and over in chorus until it ceased making sense and our English teacher lost her (now that I look back on it, considerable) patience yet again and threatened us, albeit with some small hint of appreciation that we actually knew what a dictionary was, with various reprisals if we didn't sit down and shut *up*. Then we'd all spend the week watching out for how often Our Word surfaced as we went about our usual activities.

Not too surprisingly, the weekly word did pop up here and there, as I recall the results of this playful little sport, which was perfectly explainable as the result of priming the perception pump. We were aware of the word, so we picked it out of our surroundings, a simple enough equation. Still, there was a particular set of connections involving the word "eleemosynary" that sticks in my mind as looming somewhat larger than chance or suggestion. It was, like the rest, chosen on the fly, as a lark, somebody's finger jamming down on the page; nothing more serious than that. But it was such a funny-sounding word, previously unknown to us, that we went nutty over it, and carried on and on, joking and yukking it up throughout class, eleemosynary this and eleemosynary that and driving it, as teenagers are so good at doing, right into the ground.

The disconcerting thing was that "eleemosynary," a relatively unusual word you hardly ever see or hear in ordinary language use, suddenly began appearing all over the place in the extracurricular lives of that little group of pals. It was in the New York Times crossword puzzle the following Sunday, for example—my mother always finished the Sunday Times puzzle (in ink, no mistakes), and sometimes I'd look it over and contribute a letter or two in humble pencil—and that week, there it was, already penned in my mother's hand, the answer to the clue for a word meaning "charitable."

Then a couple of my friends said they'd heard the word on a TV quiz show that week, asking for its definition; another claimed that a family member had actually used it in a sentence, having nothing to do with the quiz show and not knowing anything about our dictionary game beforehand (which admittedly strains credibility a tad, but this is how I remember it). Somewhere, in something I picked up to read around that time, probably in the weekly New Yorker, which my mother subscribed to, I came across That Word yet again, which wouldn't have been atypical in that magazine, though the timing of that week was what caught my attention. Had I ever come across it in those pages before this? I couldn't remember. Yet it was an odd word, and I liked odd words, collected them as it were—would I have noticed it out of context without our dictionary hijinks? I can't say.

There were several other instances I don't remember specifically now, just the sense that they occurred, and the surprise this generated among us. Moreover, I have a strange but vivid image of the bunch of us driving around Elmira and seeing the word on a sign! The local A&W Root Beer stand, a favorite stop, colors this picture, though I hardly think A&W (or anyone else) would have put "eleemosynary" up on its billboard, so this is probably a half-remembered dream—charming, and possibly even a precognitive "hit" back then, though there's no way for me to know, as I didn't start keeping dream journals until after I was out of college and my high school friends had long since scattered in the winds of life.

Since I have no records of these forty-two-year-old events and only the most fleeting of memories, there's really nothing much to say about what was overall a thing of passing remark, except as a reminder of good times—and that it is evocative of something else, of something about the workings of the conscious mind and the reality in which it dwells, and the relationship that exists between the contents of each, that later came to fascinate me so much. It is also very much like the "daily prediction" lists I kept for a while in the sixties. These lists, which are fun and easy to do, display an exquisite open-ended hint at what the "perception pump" might actually be up to, and capable of perceiving. Tests, as it were, measuring what you know, and when it is you apparently know it.

What you do is this: At some point in the day, sit quietly for a moment and scribble out a list of the first ten or fifteen things that come into your head, without any effort to think of anything specific or weed out what sounds like nonsense. Then keep track of what, if anything, connects with the items on that list over the next couple of days. Sometimes the results will startle you, to say the least. More than setting up expectations in a world full of possible associations, these lists often seem to reflect a focused sort of precognition mixed with coincidence in a most evocative way, as if catching the threshold where things emerge, or "come

true." Usually these results aren't even about anything of outward importance, and are rarely as elaborate as the "natural" coincidence-constructs
that can come at you with such mind-bending complexity. Yet the feeling of connection between these lists and the neat little offhand blips of
coincidence that rise out of them—sometimes right on, sometimes just
off the mark, sometimes its exact opposite (so exactly opposite as to seem
the same thing)—are indicative of . . . something. Something undeniably
familiar, as if whatever it is has been going on all the time just beneath
the surface of your awareness.

But what is "it," exactly? The conscious mind's desire to give
meaning to a fundamentally objective world? An attempt to assign
self-aggrandizing significance to what's little more than mathematical
probabilities? Some other inherent abilities that we ignore, disdain,
even fear?

For example, some of my old prediction lists include the following:[1]

Wednesday, February 12, 1969, 9:50 P.M.
1. short shrift of things
2. Viola
3. standing room only
4. hot fudge sundae
5. crime
6. crying spree
7. Mullin's hat
8. time to go
9. time refusal
10. good fortune

> #2 and #3?: February 13, saw line-up of bass fiddles in a
> store that impressed me.
> #4 and #5: Same day, ate first hot fudge sundae in a
> long time (sort of felt like a crime)

#5: Learned Friday P.M. that one of [my soon-to-be husband] Ned's former college roommates had been arrested for stealing. Scared me.

#6?: I cried myself to sleep Saturday P.M.

#7: Next morning, looking at list, I thought of a favorite rejoinder of my father's [Newell Mullin]: "Go shit in your hat!" Wished I could say the same about now. #1: Short shrifting myself? (Ned and I married, reluctantly, on February 25.)

Wednesday, July 2, 1969, 7:50 A.M.
1. traveler's cheque
2. The Iron Bar
3. handsome carriage
4. a pickle recipe
5. chloroform—sickening
6. eaten up by a grasshopper
7. a chance for a farm

#2 also #5 or #6?: That night we stopped off at an Elmira bar (unplanned) and played some pool. The place stunk like old booze, made me feel sick. A "grasshopper" is a kind of sicky-sweet drink. Connected? Also #1: Ned cashed a check in the bar and had some trouble convincing the bartender to do it (odd spelling of "cheque" a clue?) and #3?: Ned was eyeing some of the cute girls ("handsome carriages") in the place. #4 (humorously)— a pickle recipe, indeed. Humph!

Thursday, July 10, 1969, 10:45 P.M.
1. noxious odors—gas fumes from downstairs
2. arms pile-up discovered—Cuba, again?

3. broken chimney—beware of it falling
4. letter from stranger—large brown envelope
5. child from reform school
6. Janis Joplin concert
7. damn old codger, anyway
8. LeMans—raceway—spectacular happening at raceway. Ferrari mix-up?
9. standing room only

> #1: Apartment stank when I came home from work Friday. Like car fumes from street.
> #2: Arms pile-up discovered in North Vietnam (according to news).
> #4: Got pamphlet in mail Saturday A.M. from NYC maternity center—strangers to me—in large brown envelope.
> #5: Ned called his cat a "juvenile delinquent" for not coming home all day Friday.
> #6: Janis Joplin was announced Friday P.M. on radio's "Music Scene" as next week's guest artist.
> #8 and #9?: On Saturday, we went to a race at the Watkins Glen track, unplanned. Ned very enthused about the cars. We hadn't discussed this; I didn't realize there was a race on. We stood at the fence near a turn the whole time (didn't buy bleacher tickets). Very crowded. I hated it (#7?).

The interesting thing about this prediction exercise—which is like a primer for a lot of intuitive activity, including dream recall—is the variety of ways that items appear to "come true." Some are oddly inchoate in nature, giving the impression that more was going on than I noticed; and, as you can see in these excerpts, there are direct hits—quite a lot of direct hits, comparatively speaking. More than that, I get a sense, reading over these excerpts now, thirty-six years later, of an amazing density within each "random" prediction that hints at infinity, the way dream symbols can represent endless layers of meaning and association. I also see more "hits" than I did at the time, along with obvious clues to repressed feelings, unspoken opinions, directions not taken, and many other pieces of random thought as I captured them in these off-the-cuff word lists. Each list-set, or "cluster," is like a little dream, except that I was awake (though relaxed) when I wrote them, allowing myself to accept whatever my conscious mind offered up—listening to its contents.

And I use the term "allowing" for specific reason, since all of us have more or less formed the habit of pretending that such things as coincidence, random thoughts, precognition and the like are either one of two things: crazy, or accidental, in a world where anyone can be victimized by anything at any given moment. It takes some doing to disengage one's conventional exterior focus from that conviction, but it does not help us as individuals or as a world to insist on it, either. The beauty of coincidence recognition is that doing so automatically changes your perspective on this score, even if momentarily.

Some years ago, while I was collecting dreams from folks in the village of Dundee, New York, for *Dreaming Myself, Dreaming a Town*,[2] the idea came to me that dreams, whether of an overt precognitive nature or not, tended to come true in bits and pieces, with dream elements showing up in waking life, morphing back into dreams, and reappearing in the world in a sideways progression that wasn't exactly "toward" something as much as it was a development of something—something with many facets and possible pathways. Only later did it occur to me that it is in fact reality itself that "comes true by bits," with the interaction of dreams, random thoughts, impulse, and coincidence acting like bricks in the mortar; the point where consciousness enters the building. That the difference between dreaming and the awake world is in the method of focus—but the way the mind seeks out and arranges data is the same.

Of course, my dream records (and yours, if you keep them) are also full of dreams and coincidences that don't seem to mean anything, or "go" anywhere. But what if this isn't a result of accurate versus not-accurate, or proof of the idea that dreams are so much brain-lint, but rather the result of how little in our waking moments we consciously observe, or can observe?

Say you're looking at a painting. To one degree or other you see what's on the surface—the colors, the objects, the scene. Oranges and grapes on a chair. A nude woman descending a staircase. Boats on a lake. All very nice. But if you have some background in art appreciation, you might see more—the brush strokes, the use of light, the depths suggested by underpainting, and other techniques not immediately available to the everyday eye. Even less apparent, if not invisible, is the undersketch that the artist may have penciled on the canvas, or the figures and shapes she might have painted over as she changed her mind or made mistakes; or maybe the artist decided to paint over an entire landscape to create a new one. Furthermore, there are alternate versions of the work that the artist set aside: the different poses considered, the minute choices of light and shadow; endless rearrangements of items to convey exactly the right feeling, various expressions on the face of the model, and so forth. Some of these were "used." Many more were not.

Except that on some level, the observer would be aware of those hidden figures and colors and the artist's changing intentions, and of the other possible paintings suggested by the finished piece. All of those elements, whether they "came true" or not in the objectified painting, would exist within it, as much a part of the work as the actual layers of paint. Or think of what happens in a novel, where the writer is aware of every direction these unruly fictional people *could* take, the words they *could* say, and of other, parallel stories that could be told if you didn't have to pick one and one only in order to make sense on the printed page. Consciously or not, the reader would be aware of those other tales and directions. Where paintings or stories or notes in a composition do *not* go is as much a part of the oeuvre as where they do, and of what we perceive within them.

Thus it is with dreams, predictions, coincidence, clairvoyance, and all the other underlying facets of consciousness, all "coming true" as psychic underpaintings that we might not observe, or that we discard, but which exist within and affect our experience nonetheless. So what I'm looking at in things like coincidence clusters is more than the amazement of the tales themselves. I'm searching out glimpses into the way reality is constructed, and the formation of that structure as it's being put into place.

A neat idea, and one admittedly fraught with all kinds of potential for boogery and bunkum, as a glance through the various websites devoted to conspiracy theories of coincidence readily proves. In that, what I'm not going to do here is delve into the large, mass-event urban-legend assemblages such as the factoids allegedly connecting the assassinations of John F. Kennedy and Abraham Lincoln, for example, where too much of the claimed information is spurious or misleading.[3] I'm as intrigued as the next person by the twists of history, and I don't discard any coincidence trail as totally worthless, but there's a balance to be maintained here, not to mention a certain decorum, as with the events of September 11, 2001. Individual dreams and coincidences about such things, sure; extrapolating omens from numerical oddities and folded dollar bills, no.[4] If there are any conspiracies to be rooted out of disaster, this book isn't the place to do it (and I find it interesting that coincidence is so often equated with conspiracy in the pejorative sense, rather the same way dreams are often pejoratively assumed to be sex dreams and precognition associated with demeaning fortune-telling stereotypes).

No, my interest here is in the personal point of view, which is the only point from which any of us can begin to make sense of the larger world, not to mention the private one we often inhabit so uneasily.

3

Lonesome Kangaroo Mama Blues
Coincidence as Parable (and the Google Mind at Work)

It's April 1997 and I'm minding my friend Kathy's antiques shop for the day, so I stop by her house in Dundee to pick up the key on my way to Penn Yan, some twelve miles north, where the store is located. She's not going to be home, so our arrangement is that I'll just go in the unlocked back door and pick the store key off her dining-room table, which I do. Thank you, small-town nonchalance!

I had owned this house briefly, from 1984 to 1986, and sold it to Kathy in a chaotic three-way moving upheaval, with me consolidating it and my parents' place into my new digs while Kathy was moving herself and two daughters to Dundee. As a result, I left some of my belongings there, mostly in the large barn out back, where they stayed for months after I'd moved out and Kathy had moved in. Later I retrieved most of them, but as often happens, some of my possessions in transit from here to there and everywhere vanished off the face of the earth.

Now as I pull out of Kathy's driveway, I gaze at the upstairs windows where my son Sean's bedroom had once been, and for no specific reason of connection or logic find myself thinking about the Steiff kangaroo I've had since childhood. That kangaroo had originally come with a small velvet baby in its pouch, but this little critter was among the items lost somewhere along the moving trail (I still have the adult, a bit floppy-eared and worn but cute as well as collectible). Sitting in my car, remembering that Steiff kangaroo baby, I imagine it lying up there in Sean's old room, shoved under a bed gathering dust, alone and forgotten. These images become more and more brilliant and detailed as I back onto the street and drive out of Dundee toward Penn Yan, and suddenly I feel so woefully, mournfully sorry for that little stuffed baby kangaroo that I start crying over its memory, wishing I had it back, stuffed safe and sound inside its stuffed old mother's stuffed pouch. Stuffed animals! So sad and forlorn! Tears roll down my face. I grope for a tissue, blow my stuffed-up nose; think about the kangaroo, cry some more. Some shopkeeper! What a mess!

So I'm motoring along, sniffling and honking, feeling simultaneously miserable and stupid, car wobbling drunkenly, and about halfway to Penn Yan I come across a huge yard sale spread out across at least a dozen tables chock-full, one of the first and biggest I've seen so far this year. Impulsively, I pull off the road, wipe my eyes, and get out; and as I cross the road and walk into the lawn, a box marked "Christmas decorations" catches my eye. For some reason, I go right to it.

Which is odd, because I don't care much for Christmas decorations and never buy any—I have piles of them from childhood but don't even decorate for Christmas any more, and I certainly have no interest in someone else's used ones. Nonetheless, I make a beeline for this box, and the first thing I see when I peer down inside it is a little hanging ornament shaped like a kangaroo, obviously hand-made, cut out of felt, with a teeny-weeny kangaroo baby in its pouch holding an even teenier green Christmas tree in its paws. Ten cents. I pick it up and pay for it, get back in my car, hang it from the rear-view mirror . . .

. . . And suddenly there I am gawping at it, stunned. The coincidence between my just-previous weepy thoughts and this yard sale find hadn't occurred to me until this instant. Grabbing the ornament was an impulse out of nowhere, with no conscious thought whatsoever, as if its meaning existed in a cordoned-off portion of my awareness, held in abeyance for maximum impact. All I can do is stare at the little kangaroo and its speck of a baby, hanging there in front of me, as the coincidence emerges. I feel this process happen physically, a sensation passing from one way of observation to another, a slow grasping of something small but remarkable and yet completely natural, nothing odd about it at all.

Well, okay, maybe it wasn't so odd—except that I had never stopped at that particular house for anything (and thus had no conscious foreknowledge of the sale's contents), and certainly had no reason to stop there that morning. By 1997 I wasn't active in the collectibles biz anymore and only had a few dollars with me anyway (from which I'd have to buy coffee and lunch), not to mention that I was running tight for time to get to Kathy's shop, another seven or eight miles away.

And not just a kangaroo ornament, either, but a kangaroo *with a baby in its pouch*! Suddenly it was like a dam bursting, the connection with my thoughts and yearnings for that velvet baby kangaroo, and the images I'd manufactured so vividly of the big stuffed mama's empty pouch, and the feelings of loss I imagined that mama kangaroo must feel. So exactly which mama was feeling sad about her baby not being close to home anymore, eh? At that point in time, Sean had been living in the southwest for nearly a decade, and I saw him maybe once a year, at Christmas time, when I flew out to visit, and not every Christmas, at that. And here's this Christmas ornament find! My worked-up mush about the lost kangaroo baby had started with a glance at Sean's old bedroom windows, after all. So what was this (very striking, and also rather funny) coincidence about? A response to some empty-nest feelings I'd become used to ignoring?

And if that were the case, what then? Did this mean that in answer to my momentary lament, some portion of my consciousness had leaped out ahead of me as I drove along, scoured through yard-sale objects along the way until it came across the kangaroo ornament, then telegraphed the impulse to stop at that particular place plus the directive to look inside that particular box so I could find that particular doodad, despite all the practical reasons for me to keep going straight though to Penn Yan?

Well, okay, sure, but—Either I was reading messages in wads of cloth (and how far was that from seeing the Virgin Mary in potato chips?) or some inherent capability of mind and matter had just responded to me in a complex layering of metaphor and—and something like good will, actually. Like a dream, I thought. If this had been a dream, the interpretation would be fairly obvious, at least to me, because of course I understood the interconnected symbolism of empty pouches and babies long gone to begin with. So maybe this *was* a dream. Or something like it, but focused in the waking world. A surmise out of the fantastic—and yet that was my feeling about it as I started my car and headed down the highway, the kangaroo dangling (happily?) from my mirror. A story to be told, to be sure: a coincidence gift, from the gods of junque.

Four years later, in November of 2001, the point is strangely updated when I come across the notes I made on this incident of the kangaroo kid. It's the first time I've looked at this tale since I wrote it up, on the same day it happened in 1997, in the spiral notebook I carry with me for such emergencies. Now I spend several minutes thinking about how wild that whole thing was, finding that little ornament in the yard sale, and while I'm reading these notes and thinking these thoughts I'm looking right at the kangaroo in question, dangling from the top shelf of my workroom bookcase where I'd hung it four years ago.

For some reason as I muse along, possibly the snow falling outside and the upcoming Christmas season with my son still far away from home and the events of September 11 so recent, I decide on impulse to email my writer friend Kitty Myers and arrange a shopping date at the big national-chain bookstore on the mall near Elmira. I rarely "shop" and hate driving anywhere in winter, but today it seems an antidote for a lot of things, and maybe fun besides. Kitty is always good-natured and upbeat despite some ongoing domestic issues that would flatten most people, and her cheery practicality bolsters the heart.

We meet the next day, blab for half an hour or so over coffee, and then go in the bookstore to browse. First place we head is the calendar section—they always make for good Christmas presents, we agree. As we stand there looking over the calendars, it spontaneously comes to me to tell Kitty I'd like to find another moose calendar like the one I bought for myself the previous year. There isn't a moose calendar here on the racks, and no moose pictured anywhere else I'm aware of, so I don't know what reminds me of this, exactly, except that I'm thinking of Sean and I add aloud that my son might also enjoy something as humorously outré as a wall calendar full of moose photos.

"Whoa," Kitty says. "Funny you should say that." She then proceeds to tell me that she always gives Christmas-tree ornament moose figures to her son-in-law as presents. Sometimes she makes these herself, she says, and sometimes she finds them at yard sales, or sometimes she buys them new, but she always manages to find a moose ornament somewhere. "I haven't found any yet this year so I guess I'd better start making a couple," she says. "I wouldn't want to disappoint my son-in-law!"

Of course immediately I'm thinking—Wow! Just yesterday I was reading over my old notes about the hand-made kangaroo Christmas-tree ornament I found in a yard sale, and as soon as Kitty stops to take a breath I jump in to tell her about this little glyph, nothing really big, but cute nonetheless; kangaroos and moose being rather unusual animals to associate with Christmas ornaments, after all. But Kitty is truly amazed by this, and her expression is one of genuine epiphany, as if I'd just given her an answer to the mysteries of the universe.

And suddenly there it is, all at once, right in front of me as we stand there in the crowded bookstore: the common thread, weaving through all of this. Kitty's position and mine as mothers of children who've left the nest in various configurations; for me, two sons separated from me by many miles; for her, issues with another kind of distance. In the middle, rising up in an unavoidably noticeable metaphor, a coincidence of ornaments shaped like ungainly (perhaps unruly) animals, and a connection with the season most affiliated with family life. For the first time it occurs to me that coincidence, and the elements of precognition and clairvoyance that exist within its borders, might exist as psychological morality plays, at the core of which is a purpose all its own.

Once you start paying attention to this sort of thing, it quickly becomes apparent that coincidence is never ambiguous. Unfailingly, it gives you the sensation of waking up from an important-feeling dream. You're supposed to take note here; something has just *happened*. Risen up, as it were, from *somewhere*. But from where? And why?

And it's more than something happening, and then something else happening that's like it or suggestive of it. Plenty of "like" things occur without that charged sense of significance about them, and to force significance on everything is to fall prey to the Texas sharpshooter fallacy (she shoots at the side of a barn and then draws a bull's eye around the holes). We're set up to recognize patterns and to retain their meaning for a lifetime—language, clothing, food, traffic, social mores, nearly everything, in fact. So the recognition of arrangement and design in itself is not what you would call paranormal; it represents part of our basic psychological make-up. It's not the totality of that make-up, however—far from it. What I'm examining here is the idea of pattern recognition as something emblematic of the psyche's larger capacity—and that drawing circles around the bullet holes may be part of the process, intuitively speaking.

You read something in a newspaper and that day find it mentioned in several different forms on the Internet; you can't get your garage door to open up and later see a funny ad on TV for garage openers featuring stuck doors; you become interested in a certain make and model car and suddenly everybody's driving one. All examples of pattern recognition, nothing more extraordinary than the result of living in a pool of constantly emerging information.[1] The difference is that the charged coincidences (the center stage, as it were) tend to appear out of the blue in overt clusters, with a loose sort of parable at the core and often with a definite beginning and end to the cluster unit, as with my encounter of moose and 'roo. At a certain moment in the bookstore, the play was done (and I could feel that it was); Kitty and I had exchanged something, or derived something that on some level was meant to impart insight to each of us, like a shared dream.

Which is not unlike Carl Jung's idea of the collective unconscious,[2] in which coincidence, dreams, and other psychological events open doors to restorative, archetypal truths. Among other things, Jung wanted to address the relationship between the individual and human culture as a whole, and thus saw the collective unconscious as a deeply hidden shared library of symbols, or archetypes, with fixed meanings and insights. Discover the archetype in any given synchronicity, as Jung called them, and you could discover the meaning of the experience.

Except that I'm not so sure there is any such thing as a fixed archetype, or that the meaning inherent in anything is buried any deeper than the top of your head; nor do I think there's a pre-formed reality, either psychologically or in the exterior world. Either consciousness rises out of form, or form rises out of consciousness—or some combination of the two, building one upon the other, in the midst of which we gather information and serve it up to ourselves in a constant fomenting exchange. The trick is in catching this process as it happens, and using that insight to better understand the conscious mind's role in creating those events—and by inference, all events, individually and en masse.

Obviously this requires a balance more exquisite than high-wire walking. You can go off the deep end too easily, especially when you try to bend everything to suit a pre-held belief, whether it's in psychoanalysis or the existence of UFOs, or even in the lack of meaning. Of course nobody escapes bias, or inclinations of opinion, and there's no reason to believe that we're supposed to. Striving to avoid Texas sharpshooting at all costs can lead you out of credulity but land you in a dried-up mechanical universe where nothing means anything, a credulity all its own. The only ideology more hopeless than that is assigning everything to the whims of an inscrutable deity. *Neither extreme takes into account the intent of consciousness, nor looks at reality as an expression of that intent.*

Granted, we are more awash in information and the sheer infinity of available details than we were, say, a hundred years ago, thus making the statistical chances of coincidence more probable, at least in terms of media spread. But what does this mean in terms of consciousness itself? Before the printed word, humans lived in a world filled with another type of information, perhaps less objectified as we think of data today, but its relationship to the individual's ability to survive had an intensity unimaginable to us now (you hardly ever get eaten by tigers while surfing the Net), and the conscious mind used natural significance in a way we've forgotten, or no longer find useful. Appreciation of available information, and the subjective framework in which it was examined, might have resulted in as much chance for noticing coincidence as there is today, where there is so much more racket, at least as we currently define it.

In this vein, you could think of Google as an exteriorized form of the conscious mind—an invented expression of how we sort through data and organize them, using connective, even random material to "attract" desired information. Using this analogy, Google's sorting capability would be like the natural act of precognition, the element of our psyche that knows what's important to us and can retrieve that information in many forms, including sets of charged patterns. The resulting coincidence "parable" would illustrate, by association, the central issue that called up one's precognitive radar in the first place. As in, finding empty-nest comfort. Or an excuse to hie yourself out of the house once in a while to escape the winter blahs. It doesn't have to be obscure!

A mouthful, I realize (maybe even a barn-side full). Still, the idea of coincidence as charged particle has a certain logic. As with prediction lists, deciding to pay attention to the question automatically becomes part of the answer. This holds true for any experiment, whether looking for correlations or living a life in the physical universe. We can't detach ourselves from our own consciousness. We have to live in a loosely agreed-upon linear world, or all would be chaos. Yet that agreement lies atop a construct that is purely intuitive, a literally endless amalgam of buried knowledge, hunches, clairvoyance, and dreams. It's up to our intellects to keep all this sensible; but our intellectual appreciation doesn't have to go it alone, and given its due can easily accommodate the intuitive origins of whatever information we might perceive.

And sometimes that information jolts our intellects like a well-timed kick in the pants.

4

It's a Small-World Surprise
Coincidence as Fork in the Road

My son Sean tells me this story, in 1997, by phone, from his house in Arizona: After weeks of calling up and nagging the owner of an engineering company just outside of Tempe, Sean finally landed a job interview for a trainee position to fly radio-controlled drone airplanes for various projects, including geological surveying, map-making, and other related tasks. The company had placed a one-day ad in the Phoenix newspaper and Sean was apparently the only respondent, so he was pretty excited about this prospect.

Sean's interest in the subject stems from, among other things, his pilot training at Sky Harbor airport in Phoenix and his undergraduate studies in geology and anthropology at Arizona State. He also has something of a background in remote-controlled airplanes from his teen years in and around Dundee, when he and his pal Jim would fly and crash these gizmos in various gleeful (occasionally flaming) formations. The two also spent the summer of 1994 building elaborate multi-stage rockets of ingenious design, which they exploded in the skies over (and occasionally on the roof of) my house. Throughout, they bought their supplies from a hobby shop in the nearby village of Odessa, where all sorts of related goods, including the components for radio-controlled airplanes and rocket motors, are stocked by the merchant, who is what you might call a singular character indeed. This fellow, whom I'll call Mr. Hobby Shop, also sells computers from his eclectic stockpile of wares, and by 1997 I'd been buying computer supplies from him for a couple of years.

So on the phone this April day, Sean says that he drove out into the desert to this engineering company and met with its owner, who as they conversed began to remind Sean more and more, and not altogether pleasantly, of a computer programmer back in Watkins Glen, New York, also an unusual though somewhat difficult character, that he and Jim had worked for in 1994, during the same summer they'd spent building and blowing up homemade rockets. And as Sean's interview continued he found himself thinking more and more about this connection, and he began to wonder if despite his interest in remote-controlled airplanes he really wanted to work for this company, and at the exact moment this question passed through his mind, the door to the office opened up and in walked Mr. Hobby Shop from Odessa, New York!

Sean, as you might guess, nearly fell off his chair in surprise. Turned out that Mr. Engineering Company and Mr. Hobby Shop had known one another since the late eighties, when Hobby Shop guy had sold a line of the company's model airplanes at trade shows, the same time frame in which Sean and Jim became interested in the things, though back then neither Sean nor Jim had heard of, or met, Engineering Company fellow.

But it just so happened that Mr. Hobby Shop was vacationing in the southwest with his family and decided to make an unplanned stop to say hello to his old friend—not only on the same day, and at the same time that Sean had finally managed to wangle his way into that office after weeks of trying, but at exactly the same moment that Sean had been thinking about his rocket-blasting summer, three years before, in which Mr. Hobby Shop's store had played such a supporting role, and the connections between those days, his old job with the exasperating computer programmer, and this job possibility now.

Mr. Hobby Shop had no idea that Sean lived in Tempe, and for that matter had no specific memory of Sean, who recognized him, and not the other way around; and indeed, Hobby Shop guy attached no particular significance to this chance meeting when Sean explained it to him there in the office. What the surprise visit did achieve was an effective end to Sean's interview, so he excused himself and left so the two friends could catch up. He never heard from Mr. Engineering Company again, which, as Sean said to me, was indicative of everything he'd been picking up on anyway.

Later, back in New York, Hobby Shop told me that he'd decided on the spur of the moment to drop in that day, without calling ahead to warn his friend, who had no idea Hobby guy was even in the southwest, let alone driving out into the desert to have a visit.[1] And not just any friend coming out to visit, either, but the friend who'd sold model and remote airplane parts and rocket components 2,500 miles and three years ago to the person sitting in the chair in front of the person that Mr. Hobby Shop was dropping in to visit. And neither Hobby Shop guy nor Mr. Engineering Company knew the computer programmer, who had played an invisible though central role in Sean's misgivings just before the door opened up and the flow of ongoing events changed its course.

More than that, which is pretty astounding in itself, the particular configuration of that moment when the door opened on Sean's interview could not have been more instantly metaphoric had this scene occurred in a bright and shining dream. For Sean it was as if a triumvirate of characteristics coalesced and took form right before his eyes: his intuitive connection between Mr. Engineering Company and the programmer from back home who'd given Sean and Jim jobs that summer of 1994, and the sudden arrival of Mr. Hobby Shop from back home, and the vague disregard for Sean's presence that followed. Despite everything that had initially seemed so ideal to Sean about this prospect, here was information demonstrating otherwise. (Considering all this later, Sean thought it interesting to remember that in 1994 the computer programmer had offered Jim and Sean permanent jobs, which Jim had accepted while Sean had moved back to Arizona.)

And it wasn't that the three men were alike, exactly—Sean didn't know any of them well enough to say one way or the other—it was more his intuitional radar connecting them than what you might call true-to-life comparison. The point is that in the moment of that coincidental event, a pertinent piece of information, floating just beneath the surface, suddenly jumped into focus and gave Sean feedback exactly when he needed to have it.

In dreams, this sort of thing is common: various people can stand for certain issues, or layers of an issue, and are often combined in a single figure to represent many facets of that issue. This can be literal, like a warning of something to come. Or it can be symbolic, offering insight into how one's own characteristics, for example, might come into play under certain conditions. All of which is often a challenge for the intellect to sift through on its own (as we usually think it must).

Did this coincidence, therefore, serve to push Sean's life into another direction? Had Mr. Hobby Shop not shown up, would Sean have gotten the job, gone who knows where with it? It's impossible to know, though he thought the interview was going quite well until the moment Hobby Shop burst into the room; in fact he'd been convinced Mr. Engineering Company was going to offer him the position. But aside from his growing intuitive doubts, Sean was uncomfortable with some of the applications of remote airplane surveying, so it's possible he wouldn't have taken it anyway, though it fit his interests and background to a tee. Nonetheless, it wasn't long after this that Sean decided to go back to school for a Master's degree in urban environmental planning, and moved to another city to pursue job prospects in that area.

Fortune-changing coincidence appearing at pivotal moments in fable and history is an old, even archetypal, idea, usually interpreted as meddling from whichever of the gods (including new-age versions) are in vogue, or as pure happenstance, nothing more. But coincidence, like dreams, has a way of expressing events that can only partly appear in physical reality, or in linear time. It's as if entire units of understanding, constantly and instantaneously updated in a vast intuitive theater of consciousness, can't "fit" in the waking moment (or at least in our ordinary focus within it), so we see representations of these units in the form of coincidence (and other paranormal) dramas. That elusive tip-of-the-iceberg feeling that so often accompanies synchronicity speaks true. The iceberg is an infinite one, formed in the seas of our own inner knowledge, where everything resides.

In that, coincidence would act like a reference point, or present metaphors for boundless resources of information, and enlarge upon them in a way that isn't otherwise possible. This is why coincidence has the impact it does, and why it often seems to come in clusters of self-referral, with repeating central themes and objects, like recurring dreams in the waking world. Like dramas set up by ourselves, using an interweave of intuitive and cognitive abilities.

So what was the interweave among these men that led to this "chance" meeting at a vortex in Sean's life? Did it involve some sort of Mount Olympus–like telepathic tribunal, mulling the direction this bright young man should take, and how he should be influenced to take it? Or was this a coincidence rising from Sean's own inner committee, shaping a string of small decisions involving phone call persistence and the timing of his drive out to the engineering firm, as it sorted through the possibilities of direction and purpose?

Maybe all Sean wanted at that point in time was the exercise of holding his own in the face of conflicting attractions, or to explore the question of what we're supposed to take from encounters like this one, and how much of our well-being depends on making use of opportunities thus afforded. Because it's possible that the mere act of recognizing the sensation of significance that rises out of coincidence, and asking what it means in the larger context of daily life, automatically enriches experience whether or not you "use" the information supplied.

Though sometimes that information is so breathtaking, and yet so convoluted and squirrelly, you can barely make any linear sense of it at all, let alone get a grasp on where it might be heading.

5

Random Thoughts, Media Feedback
The Structure of Modern Coincidence

June, 2004: I've been reading Max Byrd's novel, *Shooting the Sun*,[1] over the past couple of days. Set in the American West in 1840, mixing historical and fictional characters, it tells the story of an expedition that sets out to take daguerreotype pictures of a predicted solar eclipse near the Santa Fe trail. It's a good tale, full of science lore of the times, but about halfway through I lose my patience with it for some reason and start skimming through the chapters to see how it comes out. So I'm not reading it consecutively when I realize at some point in my flooffing that the novel's characters are talking about the weather theories of a "cloud scientist" named Luke Howard.

What catches my eye about this reference is that I'm pretty sure this must be the real-life person who's the subject of Richard Hamblyn's *The Invention of Clouds*,[2] which I read soon after Sean gave it to me for Christmas two years ago. I can't quite remember the actual cloud-namer's name, though—I'm running on an intuitive hunch about it—so I pick Hamblyn's biography off my bookshelf and sure enough, same guy. The next day, I open my new copy of Bill Bryson's 544-page *A Short History of Nearly Everything*[3] completely at random, and my eyes fall on this: "The person most frequently identified as the father of modern meteorology was an English pharmacist named Luke Howard, who came to prominence at the beginning of the nineteenth century. Howard is chiefly remembered now for giving cloud types their names in 1803." Cute!

Note the connecting element here not just of Luke Howard's name and specific subject reference, but my arbitrary skip-throughs that produced the coincidence-thing in the particular progression of time (one right after the other) and reference (to a historical person-age I had never heard of before reading Hamblyn's book). Of course eclectic-reading cross-reference happens all the time, and anyone who reads a lot, as I do, expects this and is more or less used to it; and since I don't bother to jot them all down, I forget many of them. Still, they don't often appear in such quick succession as this one. Maybe the cloud reference strikes me the way it does because of the ongoing lit-tle humorous jabs about fiction versus nonfiction that Sean and I indulge (he has little tolerance for modern fiction), and in that regard it's funny that *Shooting the Sun*'s fictional characters discuss a real-life person from a book Sean sent to me and then that person turns up the next day in my perusal of Bryson's book, which is what you might call a mega-travelogue of nonfictional time.[4] Plus, I have a mini-hobby photographing cloud formations and like to imagine what clouds are thinking about as they trundle toward various destinations across the sky. So clouds hold a storyteller's attraction (as well as nature of con-sciousness rumination) for me to begin with.

Beyond that, this kind of synchronistic intercorrelation with print and electronic media interests me as a structure, precisely because it's a relatively recent one in the history of human conscious-ness. You would think that the sheer volume of available information would accelerate the chances of seeing such coincidences; that we'd be bombarded with them almost to the exclusion of every other kind of sense data. Yet this doesn't seem to happen as often as you or I might suppose. In a way, and admittedly contrary to how statistics work, I sometimes wonder if the amount of exterior data available to modern senses doesn't actually dilute the probability of coincidence rather than make them more, well, probable—as if the conscious mind's sorting capabilities would need to shut out half the racket overload just to stay on course. On the other hand, the racket itself is an invention of the human mind, so it comes to us pre-approved, and its structures intuitively understood, however chaotic they might appear. Within, coincidence rises up out of the babble in perfectly smooth response to your natural interests and inclinations. Not to mention what you need to hear. To wit:

July, 2004: I'm taking a shower in my apartment around 11 A.M. when I remember that I didn't lock, or even close, the front door, which has been wide open all morning in the summer air, and I didn't throw the lock button on the screen door, either. I'm not particularly bothered by this; it seems comical to me more than anything, so typical of my obliviousness to town living, some of which comes from years in an isolated rural house with a dog who always sat across from the bathroom door as I showered, barking frenzy at the ready if anyone dared come near. But I also feel perfectly secure in my new place. The bathroom is in the back of the apartment, tucked around the corner of the kitchen, and the front door is shielded from the sidewalk by a wraparound porch and tall bushes. It just didn't cross my mind to close and lock the front door before stepping in the shower.

I'm thinking about all this as I start washing my hair, and as I stand there, water running down my face and the quasi-translucent shower curtain giving the bathroom a certain spectral light, I suddenly remember all too vividly the famous shower scene from "Psycho" with Janet Leigh in the role she's most noted for in her career. Great, here I am in the shower, thinking about Janet Leigh getting stabbed in the shower. But then my thoughts move smooth as soap to another old movie of hers I saw years ago, something about Vikings—was it called "The

Vikings?" Yes, I think, it was. And as I finish rinsing my hair, I ruminate on my vague memories of this film, which center on the beautiful costumes, especially Janet Leigh's, which I remember clearly even though I haven't seen the movie since the late fifties, when I was a teenager.[5] With that my (uneventful) shower is done.

Later that afternoon I drive out to friend Dave's house to watch the 7:00 Yankees game on the YES channel. Dave's at work and I'm early for the game so I decide to scroll through the dish schedule to see what else might be on—and whaddya know! There on the Action channel is none other than "The Vikings," with Tony Curtis, Kirk Douglas, and Janet Leigh! I cannot remember coming upon so much as a tagline about this movie since I saw it forty-something years ago. Of course it's possible that it's been offered before today on the satellite package Dave subscribes to, but since I don't have a TV anymore (I gave mine away when I moved into my apartment), I don't read program schedules unless I'm at his house.

I watch the movie for a few minutes, decide it's a lot cheesier than I remembered (though the costumes are still beautiful), and after writing a sentence or two in my notebook about this coincidence I go back to scrolling—and funny thing, and almost peripherally, I notice that "The Puppet Masters"[6] is on the Mystery channel at 8:00. Unlike "The Vikings," I've watched "Puppet Masters" at least twice since its debut in 1994, and have seen it listed on the various dish channels probably half a dozen times in the past few months—but the thing is that just two days before, I started reading Carl Zimmer's absolutely flabbergasting *Parasite Rex: Inside the Bizarre World of Nature's Most Dangerous Creatures*,[7] and had just this morning finished reading the chapter in which Zimmer talks about the portrayal of parasites in sci-fi films, dwelling in particular on "The Puppet Masters," in which parasitic aliens control the minds of their hosts (as do some real-life Earthly parasites, as Zimmer describes with great enthusiasm). *Parasite Rex* had been sitting on my bookshelf for a couple of months before I picked it

out to read day before yesterday. I have dozens of books in my apartment, a combination of old favorites, some recent purchases, and the
usual pile of library books. My choice of Zimmer's was completely on
impulse, an arbitrary grab.

So here's a funny blend of shower thoughts about a movie I haven't
seen in years, and up it pops on TV; a book I'm reading that mentions
a sci-fi flick I've seen several times, which pops up on TV on the same
night (and in the same Encore movie package). Some dovetailing here
I can't quite grasp, some connection with past and present, and the
interrelation of thought processes. But try as I might, I can't define
what it is about this set of correlations that intrigues me so much.
Really, it's hardly super-remarkable fare, and yet—something about it
feels unfinished, is what it is. Open-ended. Still *becoming*.

One thing I've noticed about coincidence clusters is that they seem
to appear in relatively short bursts with a definite beginning and an end-
ing, though the clusters themselves can connect, and often do, with
other clusters, or units of coincidence, days, and even years, afterward.
Sometimes this wormhole effect is an obvious benefit of heightened
awareness. Other times it seems to come out of the blue, on its own,
startling your attention with a definite sense of import, similar to the
experience of *déjà vu* and its siblings, *presque vu* (almost seen, almost
understood) and *jamais vu* (seeing the familiar as if for the first time).
But this group I'm noticing now isn't exactly like any of those sensations,
either. I make a few more notes, surf a little more TV, waiting for more
to come of it. Nothing does. Finally the Yankees game begins and I slip
into a pleasant baseball trance and forget the whole thing.

I forget it, that is, until three days later when I'm again out at
Dave's house, reading the Sunday *New York Times* while we're watching
another Yankees game, and I turn to the Book Review, in which there's
a lengthy piece by Allen Barra titled, "You Can Observe a Lot by
Watching,"[8] a review of seven recently issued baseball books. In the
past, I wouldn't have given this sort of article a second glance, but I've

become a devoted fan of baseball in recent years and enjoy watching the game very much, particularly the Yankees.[9] So here I am, baseball on TV, baseball in the newspaper, and in his review of *Baseball Forever: Reflections on 60 Years in the Game* by Ralph Kiner[10] (a Hall of Fame outfielder and New York Mets announcer), Barra writes, "[Kiner] does not back down on what he regards as the myth of [former baseball general manager] Branch Rickey as the Great Emancipator," and goes on to quote Kiner as saying, "When Rickey came to the Pirates in 1950, he was in no hurry to bring in any African-American players to integrate or upgrade our team."

Then Barra writes: "[Kiner]'s tone softens when he reminisces about his love life, particularly his romance with Janet Leigh, 'a real down-to-earth girl,' he subsequently lost to Tony Curtis."

What?! A mention of Janet Leigh in a *baseball* book review, and on this specific Sunday, right after that whole thing with my random thoughts in the shower, and "The Vikings," and all that? Wow! I quickly haul out my trusty notebook and jot down the specifics so I can put this thread together later. For me, the focus of my notes is the mention of Janet Leigh. I'm not especially conversant on the history of baseball, and the name "Branch Rickey" doesn't mean anything to me.

Or anyway it doesn't until the next day, Monday, when I go to the library to pick up my reserve copy of Robert Parker's newest book, *Double Play*.[11] I know from a review in a previous Sunday *Times* that it's about the relationship between Jackie Robinson and Parker's invented ex-Marine who in the novel is hired to guard Robinson during his first year with the Brooklyn Dodgers, but that's all I know about it. It isn't until I start reading the book that evening that I realize Branch Rickey is in it, as the manager who brings Robinson to the Dodgers from the Negro Leagues, as he did, in fact, in 1947.

Funny that the library had called on Saturday to tell me the Parker book was in, but I didn't pick it up until the day after I'd read Allen Barra's Book Review article. Which means nothing in itself, except there's a feeling here of an order of events weaving through this coincidence progression, full of asides and hints of a mystery, waiting for me to focus my attention just so and solve it, or realize . . . What? Does the act of recognizing such progressions change the way they develop? What if I'd started the Parker book on Saturday? What difference would it have made?

What I had here was an oddly evocative thread: a random thought in the shower and a memorably creepy allusion in a book about internal parasites, two movies noticed on a casual TV surf while waiting for a baseball game to come on, a book review and its connection with a novel's real-life baseball character, and a mention in the book review specifically referring to my original random thought. Reading Parker's opus (which Barra doesn't mention) before the book review article would have changed all this in some way I can't put my finger on, but it's interesting that the novel's tone presents Rickey in contrast to the remarks quoted in Barra's review, for one thing. For another, *Double Play* ends with a gentle coincidence (the title itself is an entendre) that ties the story together and offers a glimpse into Robert Parker's own boyhood, and to a vanished era in America as symbolized by baseball's heyday. I'd had a reserve on the book for some weeks, and it just "happened" to come in on this particular weekend. Had I read it a month before this, or two months later, the connection wouldn't have clicked in so markedly, if at all.

Even more amusing, it wasn't until five months later when I was writing up my notes for this batch of correlations that I read past Barra's review of *Baseball Forever* and realized that the next book on his list is *The Zen of Zim* by Don Zimmer.[12] Who as far as I can tell is no relation, in the usual sense, to Carl Zimmer of *Parasite Rex*, another book with a vaguely punster title. Don Zimmer was the Yankees' bench coach for a number of years, and—here's a disturbing connection-loop for you—it was my intense curiosity about the unspecified internal parasite that sickened two Yankees players in 2004 that led me to buy Carl Zimmer's deliciously revolting book in the first place!

I don't know how "The Vikings" movie works into this—maybe the real Vikings were all infested with parasites. Then there's the figure of Janet Leigh: an actress whose career roles often seem emblematic of some troubling beliefs about women's life roles, like a subset of Marilyn Monroe's more exaggerated allegory for the same thing, all part of the times in which I also formed my ideas of what it meant to be a woman. And here in this thread is a remark about Janet Leigh's relationship with a major league baseball figure (as Marilyn Monroe also had), and here I am in midlife forming a relationship with the game of baseball, as if— what? As if to say, hey, I'm not just some old girlie-girl, see? As in, some sort of apology for my female self? And yet aside from baseball's inherent elegance, there are elements of it (or any organized sport), the back-room manly-man aspects specifically, that repel and frighten me. What a strange mix! And why this little revelation now, if that's what it's about?

In that, maybe my intuitive timing with Robert Parker's novel was meant to soften this whole equation (as in, perhaps I merely yearn for an iconic past or the ethos of team play or even, egads, television, more than I care to admit). And self-realizations are an ongoing pleasure, or should be, however they arrive in one's life. But aside from the dream-like hint of subthemes that waxes and wanes through this coincidence progression, what it also serves to illustrate is how each of us utilizes our own familiar structures to transport synchronistic events toward our conscious attention.

For example, it's not surprising that I would pick up on cross-appearing coincidence-connections in newspapers and books, given how loaded these media are with the magic and significance of my creative life. I was a newspaper reporter of mostly small-town events, and my writing endeavors overall spring from that milieu. It doesn't escape my notice that the coincidences I experience are of the same general homey atmosphere, rather than, say, mighty correlations that bounce through larger, mass events (these do appear, certainly, but usually as a kind of side-remark on the personal stuff). While it's fair to say that all of us are more or less saturated with media presence, for me the "true" venue remains the printed page, with television acting as a second-stage reflection of things already substantiated. And though I read a daily dose of Internet news, I don't experience (or am too wary to give credence to) coincidence clusters in that forum at all. The clue is that I don't like Net news, and have therefore no intuitive attachment to it as medium-media.

Thus the vocabulary of your interests determines the symbols used by your inner senses, exactly the way dreams operate. Within the safety of that framework, chosen and adapted by you, coincidence will often seem to cycle around bits and pieces that suggest themes you *should* be paying attention to, even if in small, gentle hints of no apparent consequence (as in my cluster of references to the cloud scientist). Again, this is exactly what your dreams are up to, or rather what you are up to in your dreams, even when you don't remember them consciously. In that way, coincidences are the awake-world extensions of the dream state, which says much about their dream-like quality and overwhelming surfeit of interconnection that often defies even the most determined attempts at record keeping.

Or maybe just learning to acknowledge coincidence is enough to maintain a link to the inner, natural workings of consciousness. Maybe coincidences are always there, muttering in the background, forming the Internet of our days, a media hullabaloo of their own. And when you do notice them, even peripherally, your intuitions spring to attention and force you to ask questions about your reality: What's going on here? What is it I have access to? Something? Nothing? Everything? And once you've asked those questions, you can never quite go back to thinking of your position in the world as meaningless or mechanical.

Which is something, all right. Maybe it *is* everything. Maybe it's the only true news we have, in fact.

6

Hugh and Me and Phone Calls Agree
Coincidence as Shared Waking Dream

It's the day after Christmas 1990 and this holiday season has been exceptionally fine. Sean is home for a visit, I have a happy new puppy in the house, and after a long discouragement with my writing career, which stalled not only in the marketplace but in my own head after some small success in dark fantasy fiction, I've finally gotten inside a new project. The gateways to my creative world seem to have opened once more. Life is good.

Sean is out making the rounds of old friends from high school years, so I'm blissfully settled in my workroom with coffee and typewriter when somewhere around noon, the phone rings and to my great surprise it's Hugh Wheeler, a.k.a. "Harold Wiles," as I called him in *Conversations with Seth*. Long retired from his job as manager of a local shopping mall, Hugh took much pride in his record-keeping abilities (as extolled in *Conversations*) and was as precise and clear-headed a person as I'd ever met, and a good friend to me, though we hadn't talked in about a year and a half.

"I have a very odd thing to tell you," he says by way of greeting. Hugh was not prone to collecting "odd things" willy-nilly, so when he noticed them you could be sure they'd be interesting. I grab a nearby memo pad and pencil and say, "What is it?"

Well, Hugh says, the thing is—did I remember his description years ago about his strong feelings of connection with Peter Deuel, the actor and co-star of "Alias Smith & Jones," the early-seventies TV western? Right from the first show, Deuel seemed . . . familiar. As if Hugh recognized him from . . . somewhere. Not a physical somewhere, though Deuel was in fact originally from Rochester, New York, a hundred and twenty miles north of Hugh's Elmira home. "It was something like a past-life thing," Hugh tells me, "but not exactly that, either." He goes on to reiterate his feeling (which he'd explained to me before) that this was further connected with Hugh's attachment to Bluff Point, the majestic peninsula that juts out between the branches of good old Y-shaped Keuka Lake, and to Hugh's lifelong dream of building a fly-in motel on top of this bluff.[1] "So it was definitely more than some kind of fan worship," Hugh adds, "but I never could quite define what. It was very peculiar, and strong."

Then Hugh explains that on impulse one day in 1971, after the debut of "Alias Smith & Jones," he'd purchased a large wall poster of Peter Deuel, with the intention of framing it and hanging it up in his house. "Totally unlike me to do that," he tells me, in an apologetic tone. "But then on December 31 [of 1971], Deuel was found shot to death in his Hollywood apartment. They called it an apparent suicide, though I never believed that. I always thought it was murder." In any case, the poster had become a source of embarrassment for Hugh, so he stashed it away in a closet, still in its tube, where it sat forgotten for almost twenty years. "Until yesterday," Hugh says. "And that's when the odd thing happened."

Seems that unbeknownst to him, Hugh's youngest son Chad decided to dig the Deuel poster out of its hiding place and have it framed and wrapped to give to his father for Christmas. "So there we were," Hugh says, "my wife and sons and everybody sitting around the tree opening presents, and I was in the process of ripping the paper off this great big square thing—I didn't know what it was yet—when the phone rang in the next room."

Who'd be calling on Christmas morning? No one knew. Chad got up to answer it, so Hugh stopped opening his present until Chad returned. Hugh could hear Chad's voice in the sort of one-sided conversation that goes with a wrong number, so he didn't pay much attention. But when Chad came back into the living room, "he looked as if he'd seen a ghost!" Hugh tells me. Which was nothing compared to the sensation Hugh had when Chad explained that the caller, who wouldn't identify himself, was phoning from a military base somewhere in the Midwest because he'd been given Hugh's number as the place where Jeff Deuel, Peter Deuel's younger brother, could be reached!

Scribbling as fast as I can, I say, "Holy shit!"

"Holy shit is right," Hugh replies, adding that Chad said he'd verified with the caller that Hugh's number was, in fact, the one given out for the Deuel residence, and was not a case of misdial. And the thing is, the area code for Rochester, where the Deuel family originated, was 716; Elmira's is 607, not all that similar, and none of the other number combinations were anything alike. "And when I recovered from that, I finished opening my present," Hugh says. "I guess you can just imagine!"

I'll say I can, because for one thing it reminds me of something that had happened just two days before, while I was doing some last-minute shopping in an Ithaca bookstore. By pure chance I'd come across a famous annual collection of fantasy and horror stories, mis-shelved in the store's Earth Science section, and the second I put my hand on it, I'd known my name was in there. And so it was, in reference to a couple of my previously published novellas. I'd had no idea I was going to be mentioned, and the bold of surprise that leaped out of that anthology had energized my writing life with an undeniable immediacy I hadn't felt in months. And I can hear a similar effect in Hugh's voice, which is filled with energy and humor, his mind obviously ranging through the significance of his own astonishing coincidence tale.

Only after we hang up after chatting for nearly an hour does it occur to me that out of all the people at Hugh's house that morning, the one who got up and answered the phone was Chad, who had resurrected the Deuel poster for his father in the first place. Interesting also that the whopping convolution of mix-up that created Hugh's story had as its central focus an actor known for his role as a fictional character; while over here in my world, I, the writer, had stumbled on a message, as it were, courtesy of a shelving flub, from a compilation of fictional characters. Just peripherally, it had been my son's idea to go over to that bookstore. Were Hugh and I working on something in tandem here? Did our needs somehow coincide? Or what?

I thought about all this for a while, typed up the notes I'd made of Hugh's experience, and forgot about it. Or thought I did. At least on the surface of things.

Hugh and I continued to communicate now and then through the years, either by occasional Christmas card or when he called to exchange dreams and unusual events and reminisce about *Conversations*. And though I knew that Hugh was having problems with neuropathy in his legs, becoming increasingly dependent on a wheelchair, he never complained about this, or mentioned his troubles in any way other than to frame them in the context of ideas and beliefs. But we weren't regular correspondents by any means, and several years passed without any word from him at all.

Fast forward eleven and a half years, to July 2001, and here I am watching a rerun of the "NYPD Blue" TV episode in which the character of detective Bobby Simone dies. As played by actor Jimmie Smits, Bobby comes down with a pericardial infection and ends up having a heart transplant to no avail, and with his beautiful police detective wife at his side and his police detective pals coming in one by one to say good-bye, he gives in to the inevitable and slowly begins to enter the other realm. His consciousness moves back and forth between his hospital bed and various scenes from his life, where he meets people he loves who've gone on before—his parents, an old mentor who acts as a guide, even his lost baby son who appears to him as a five-year-old.

It's all so well-written and perfectly acted and excruciating that fifteen minutes into it I'm sobbing and wailing like a pack of coyotes, and just as the music swells and Bobby slips into the invisible world forever, my phone rings and is immediately picked up by the answering machine, which I'd turned on earlier so I could enjoy myself uninterrupted. I'm blubbering so hard into a wad of tissues that I can barely hear the incoming caller, but somehow the last few words of the woman's unfamiliar voice gets through, and she's saying something like, ". . . very ill with heart problems," and recites a phone number.

This message and the TV episode end at almost exactly the same moment, and at first I'm so confused by the coincidence of timing and my overwrought state of imagination that I think somebody is calling me about Bobby Simone's death, as if it happened to a real person, not a character in a storyline. I mop my face, blow my nose, and play the message back. To my shock it's Hugh Wheeler's wife, calling to tell me that Hugh is in an Elmira hospital, indeed "very ill with heart problems," and wants me to call as soon as I can.

I'm still pretty flummoxed by all of this, but I call the number, thinking it's the one for the Wheeler house and somebody's going to tell me Hugh died, except that after five or six rings, Hugh answers the phone! He's in the hospital, all right, and his wife apparently had just called me from their house after going through a bunch of papers, at Hugh's request, to find my unlisted number. Turns out he's been there for a while—he's not sure how long—with congestive heart failure, among other troubles, "and the outlook isn't good," he says, then adds in his usual wry manner, "They might have the box built, but I'm not letting them nail down the lid just yet!" I laugh and we talk for a while. In fact, he's had quite an awful time of it lately, though his demeanor is as steadfast as ever.

He then turns the conversation to the reincarnational memoir, as he calls it, of past-life recollections and other "odd sightings" (his words) that's he's always wanted to write, much of which took place in and around the Finger Lakes, and Bluff Point in particular. "I figure if I'm gonna do it, now's the time to get to it," he says dryly. He asks my advice on what sort of word processor he should buy for the project, and also talks at length about his dreams, though he's been unable to sleep much in the hospital. "Maybe I'm afraid of running into Jane [Roberts, who died in 1984]," he says. "Maybe I think she'd only show up to escort me out!"

We have a discussion about this possibility—meeting dead people in our dreams who are there to help with the dying process—and as we talk it's of course running through the back of my mind (though I don't mention it to Hugh) that this is exactly what the "NYPD Blue" episode was about, and how interesting it is that this idea, of consciousness moving between worlds, appeared on this particular night on a network television program, and how ideas in general move inexorably from the unofficial into the official world. Also, there's a parallel of unflagging courage: the fictional Bobby's, and that of my friend Hugh, a man literally on his last legs refusing to give up his curiosity about such questions as multidimensional lives.

And all of it snapped into focus by the specific timing of his wife's words on my answering machine, mixed and muddled with that specific work of TV fiction—that connection with actors and their television roles again, as with Hugh's Christmas coincidence with Peter Deuel. As if our constructed fictional characters and dramas can be used to express not only the traditional elements of storytelling, but as individualized coincidence displays with built-in metaphors at the ready, a dazzling feat of consciousness whatever its applications might be. It all whirls around in my head. Wild, just wild.

Hugh was right about the nails in the lid: Not just yet. He eventually recovered enough to go home, at least for a while.

A year goes by. It's now August 2002 and in this morning's mail is the copy of Loren Coleman's revised edition of *Mysterious America*[2] I recently ordered. I have a copy of the original 1983 edition, but enjoyed Coleman's style so much, and his inclusion of mysterious tales from around the Finger Lakes, that I'd decided to buy the updated version. Perusing chapter 22, titled "The Name Game," I come across the following sentence: "And Watkins Glen, New York, is the site of reoccurring disappearances."

I don't recall seeing this passage in the original version, though I might have done so, certainly; but the mention of Watkins Glen (a village located on the south end of Seneca Lake, six miles from my house) and its synchronism with my last name,[3] along with passages I just finished revising in the novel I'm working on (in which I write that "people appear and disappear all the time around these hills"), plus newspaper reports of a recent local tragedy in which yet another boater fell into the waters of Seneca Lake, never to be seen again (despite the efforts of a professional recovery team)—all of this leads me to do something rather out of character for me, which is to sit down on the spot and write an email to author Coleman (who has so conveniently included his address in the back of his book), asking for some elaboration on his Watkins Glen–area disappearances remark.

Much to my surprise, Coleman not only answers my email that same afternoon, but it turns out he's heard of my own published books, and pays me some compliments thereto. He writes, "I decided to put the [mention of Watkins Glen] in the book, knowing someday it would mean something to someone. I guess that comment was waiting for you." But the information he adds about the Glen-area disappearances involves some teenagers from the seventies, and from my perspective looks as much like a runaway situation as anything, though I don't know the people or anything about the case, so I form no further opinion about it.[4] Truth is, I'm more interested in the little quincunx of connective elements from my end of it than I am in the missing parties themselves. I

send an email back to Coleman thanking him for his reply and explaining my interest in asking him the question about "The Name Game" in
the first place.

Then I break off my dialup connection (thus freeing the phone
line), and immediately—literally within seconds—the telephone rings.
It's Hugh Wheeler, whom I haven't heard from in a year; but as it was
last time—when he was in the hospital—his news is a mix of not so
great plus his usual equanimity. His health has deteriorated, and he's
about to check into a skilled-nursing facility (one not far from my
house, in fact) and wants to use the time he has left to get his beloved
memoir together. And he's called to ask me a question about *names*—
when it's okay to use real names, and when to use fake names, when
writing nonfiction.

Of course just two minutes before this, I'd sent Loren Coleman an
email specifically rooted in his "Name Game" chapter and its connection with me—but then Hugh goes on to further astound me by mentioning that somewhere in the late nineteen-seventies he'd struck up a
correspondence with the late author F. Scott Rogo, who expressed an
interest in interviewing Hugh about past-life memories and "odd sightings" for a book of that *he* was writing (though Rogo never followed
through on this, Hugh adds).

The thing is, I know from reading Coleman's book—from reading
it just this morning—that Coleman and Rogo are friends! But before I
can figure out a simple way to explain the whole Coleman connection,
Hugh goes on to tell me that Rogo had been murdered at some point
in time, he isn't sure when, which makes me think of the whole story
Hugh had told me so long ago—how long ago *was* it, I wonder, by now
almost totally befuddled—about the TV actor Peter Deuel, whose
death Hugh had always thought was murder, rather than the official
cause of suicide.

What Hugh also doesn't know—though surely this has to be mere
coincidence—is that in the late seventies I'd worked briefly as a reader

for Prentice-Hall press,[5] and one of my first assignments was to evaluate F. Scott Rogo's as-yet unpublished manuscript, "Phone Calls from the Dead"[6] (talk about strange message threads!). I don't think I'd ever told Hugh about this; I'd forgotten about it myself until that moment. But even if I had mentioned this to him back then, more than twenty years ago, there's no way Hugh could have known about today's connections with it that were now threatening to overload my circuits. It also occurs to me, distantly, as if in passing, that Hugh's memoir involves his own "odd sightings," exactly the subject that interests Coleman so much; and that moreover, the novel I'm currently revising—in which (I suddenly realize) people seem to mysteriously vanish but don't, and appear to have been murdered but aren't, the novel that was on my mind as I sent Coleman that initial email—is the one I'd started back in December of 1990, almost to the day of that first phone call from Hugh that started this connective chain between us!

As soon as Hugh and I hang up—I promise to visit him after he's settled—I email Coleman again, among other things asking after Rogo's fate. Then I scramble through my dream records and journals until I find my write-up of Hugh's story about Peter Deuel and the funny Christmas phone call in 1990, twelve years ago. The next day, Coleman replies that Rogo had indeed been murdered—twelve years ago, in August of 1990.[7]

To say that this string of coincidental contact between friends is merely a happenstance juxtaposition of timing signifying nothing, to me beggars one's intuitive common sense. For one thing the life-passage elements lying just beneath the surface of these conversations fairly radiate with significance for all of us, not just Hugh and me. But in another way the precise timing and purpose of Hugh's calls redefine the whole idea of what intuition might actually encompass. In contrast to the progression that most coincidence tales take, I was never thinking specifically of Hugh in the moments before my phone rang. Instead, the connection between us rose out of representational circumstance, a storyboard spread out invisibly beneath the years. What Hugh and I shared was the outward appearance of a multilayered, symbol-enhanced inner drama that we made use of, together and separately, in a neat choreography that meshed our individual needs—some unknown to the other, at least consciously—with common ground we could access across the bonds of friendship. Like a mutual dream—in the waking world.

And its meaning to either Hugh or me, or to anyone? Well for starters, how about the simple importance of maintaining one's courage in the face of life's impending sundown, or against the numbing onslaught of self-doubt?

Because I think it's fair to say that at least for me this cluster acted like a voice in my ear reminding me that time is short, and the water rises. Though we talked about his memoir often in my subsequent visits to him in the nursing home, Hugh never managed to finish his project. He died a year later, August 2003, at the age of 79, a brave man who faced that good night with humor and dignity.

Of Marbles, Money, and Mulch
The Duet of Imagination and Coincidence

I had this great facility as a kid: I could find marbles. I could also find money, but as any kid knows, marbles are the real treasure. Thinking of it now, it seems as if I must be remembering dreams instead of something called reality, except that I still have the marbles, dozens of beautiful milky glass ones in all colors, sitting in a jar on my desk, the dark blue "commander" agate perched on top. All I had to do, back then, as I walked along the quiet streets of my neighborhood, was imagine a marble lying in the dirt by the sidewalk, and one or two steps later there it would be, appearing in response to my thoughts, or so it felt. Mostly I found them one at a time, occasionally two or three together, not every day or even very often, because it didn't occur to me to try this more than once in a while . . . and what were they doing there, anyway? I haven't seen a marble on the sidewalk since 1956—have you? Or maybe I just don't believe they're there anymore. Once we moved out into the country, pleasant woods and fields and roadsides but no sidewalks, the marbles quit showing up.

So did the money. Not so many rural walkers with holes in their pockets, I suppose. On the other hand, there's something about imagination that we all begin to lose as we mature—a trust in it, even a willingness to depend on it. Most kids do this naturally until they're taught otherwise, especially about tricky subjects like money. You can't conjure things out of thin air!

But conjure them I did, at least for a while. As with the marble, all I had to do was imagine some money lying near the sidewalk and bang, a few steps later, there it was. Again, I didn't do this all that much; it wasn't a purposeful acquisitive thing. It was playful and funny, like pretend, and couldn't be forced. But I "knew" that if I turned my mind in a certain way, it would work. I remember ambling down the street one spring afternoon with my pal Darlene; seven or eight years old, all the time in the world on our hands, and she says something like, I wish we had some money to go to Pop's (the neighborhood store) and buy some candy, and I sweep my eyes toward the grass and say, "Money like this?" just as if I've already seen what's lying there waiting for me, because there it is: three folded dollars sticking up from the weeds.

I reach down and pick up the bills, grinning like a cat. Darlene is incredulous—almost angry. She refuses to go to the store and spend the money. "Jesus wouldn't like that," she says, in a tone that implies I've stolen the bucks from The Man himself, and maybe in some sense she's right; stolen it from the dream world, is the thought that crosses my mind. Of course, smart-mouth me says something like, "Jesus doesn't give a poop," which upsets Darlene even more, and so we part company for the day and I go home with my found treasure, or maybe I walk to the store and spend it, I've forgotten.

But what I remember clearly is that wonderful, wild feeling, funny and free, that went through me as I reached over and grabbed the money. As if anything were possible, whatever I imagined.

And what is this imagining tied to result, the "little thoughts tossed out," the random wish that connects with object or event in such startling reply? Is it something only kids have, in those brief years before they absorb the idea that this isn't how reality works? That imagination is okay as far as it goes, but not to be confused with real life? That coincidence is meaningless?

No, the fact is that this facility is always with us, despite our efforts to educate it properly. Almost without your notice, the imagination presents a never-ending moving picture of what you want and what you believe is possible, and moreover its images often "come true" in the same way precognitive dreams come true—in bursts of coincidence feedback, sometimes literally recreating the thing you imagined.

For example, there I am in the summer of 1993, not only an adult, but one who's decided to build a maze of flower beds and walkways around her house and needs a huge pile of shredded wood ships in order to do it. Problem is, there's no easy way for me to acquire them. Since my car is a hatchback, I have no means to haul anything like this myself, and don't feel I can ask anyone to lend me a vehicle, as borrowing a truck to lug heavy, filthy wood chips six miles or more on someone else's tires and springs seems too presumptuous. Hiring the job would be possible, though expensive. So after ruminating on this for a while, I give it up and imagine that the chips will somehow or other magically appear. Except for deciding where I'd put the pile, I create no special solution to accompany this—all I do is think something like, the chips will just magically appear, that's all. In my head I see them heaped on the grass, steaming and reeking of delicious rot. Then I go on to other garden chores and forget about it.

A day or two later I'm driving down the highway into Watkins Glen when I pass a group of men trimming tree branches and running them through a grinder into an enormous hopper, which is already half-full of my beloved chips. I make note of the company's phone number from the side of the trucks and decide I'll call them when I get home and ask if they could bring me a load—after all, they have to dump them somewhere, and my house isn't far from this ongoing project.

I get home about an hour and a half later, and as I'm taking grocery bags out of my car, a pickup with this tree-trimming company's logo on it comes up the driveway. The workmen, it turns out, have also been hired to prune trees near the electric lines on my property, and they're just checking in with me before they start. As we're talking, the big grinder-truck I'd noticed before pulls up by the foot of the drive, and oh my yes indeed the hopper is overflowing with wood chips, which they gladly unload in my previously-determined yard spot upon request.

Interesting little element of "cause" and "effect" involving imagination plus a touch of overt will (my decision to call the company, even though I didn't actually do it). In the eighteen years I lived in that house, this was the only time I ever had any sort of interaction at all with tree-trimmers, or anyone else, with a truckload of wood chips. (It was also the only time I wanted any, so there you are.)

It does seem, however, that the more playful one is about imagining a desired thing, the more immediate and literal the result. This could be the key reason that stuff like this works so well for children—they have no inhibitions about pretending, treating it more or less as a given in the true-and-false world. For them it's *all* true. They have no desperation about it, no constant checking to see if the pot's boiling yet. A slippery stance to hold onto consciously. Or even if you can, it takes a trick of consciousness to let yourself follow through with it in the face of logic. As on the morning I filled two large boxes with comics to take to Eddie P.'s used-book store in Watkins Glen. Same day, I have a 9:00 appointment to leave my vehicle for an oil change at the Chevy garage. I want to accomplish both errands at once, but the garage is located too far from Eddie's store to carry the boxes all the way down the long block, and I can't drop them off first because Eddie doesn't open until noon. I could leave them behind for another day, but I want the comics out from underfoot now, without having to make a special trip.

The more I try to force a solution, the more it eludes me, and before I know it, I've peeved myself into a royal gut-grinding tizzy, and over what? Five bucks worth of old moldy comics? Really, it would be funny if I weren't so annoyed. So for the hell of it I decide to imagine that some unknown thing will come along to resolve this (largely self-made) conundrum. I don't try to figure out what that thing might be—I just tell myself it will appear, and with that my sour feelings vanish. I load the boxes into my car and head for town. Chances are I'll be hauling them right back home, but I might as well pretend otherwise. Why not?

Then on the way down the driveway, I decide for some reason to stop at the nearby rural post office to mail a birthday card I have with me, rather than leave it in my roadside box for pickup. This is a vague and rather peculiar sort of impulse, since whichever I do makes no difference in whether or not the card gets to its destination on time, so why bother making the stop? Good question, but I follow the impulse anyway and when I walk into the post office who should be there but old Ralphie the antiques dealer, who as it happens (as he tells me) is clerking today in the co-op that's located right above Eddie's store!

I ask Ralph if he'd mind taking the comics into town for me, and I'll walk down from the Chevy garage and stash them in the co-op until I can catch Eddie some other time, and Ralph says, sure, whatever, no problem.

Funny how the progression of this solution-coincidence was reminiscent of the construction of my original dilemma—leave the boxes or schlep them down the street; leave the card or take it to the post office. Had I invested as much angst into the question of where to mail the card as I had in how to deliver the comics, it's possible I wouldn't have run into Ralph at all, since for one thing, the timing was quite precise— he was about to go out the post office door as I arrived. Almost as if the coincidence depended on a certain conversion of energy to transform itself across the line from something loosely imagined into something that actually happened.

These are fantastic hints at the possibilities inherent in consciousness, particularly when you consider the element of best interests that these coincidences incorporate. It's as if my childhood marble and money-gleanings were practice for a grown-up world in which one's confidence in such things is no longer as easily accessed, and requires some common-sense diligence that kids don't need to address. Even more striking is that none of these coincidence-solutions took anything even approaching what we think of as effort, and a mere eyelash in the passage of time. In these examples, I imagined the outcome according to specific need: with my wood chips, it was the item; with the comics, it was the method. Then there's the way imagination can be used to effect more complex changes, even when the imaginer doesn't want to admit she needs to change at all:

May 2004: I've been feeling sorry for myself lately. I'm living in a new town, most of my old friends are email only anymore, and I miss the sort of social interaction I used to have, back in my newspapering days for instance, or while I was working in the antiques biz. Not that I want to turn into a gadabout, but it would be nice if there were other writers or bookish folks nearby, something like that.

Over the past day or two this vague yearning has migrated up into my consciousness, and so I take a few minutes to imagine connecting with a few people, nothing definite, no clear pictures of anything; just the idea of somebody to hang out with once in a while. Typical of me, I don't want to go so far as to join a club or actively seek out people—not me! Who needs that? I'd rather make something up. If it doesn't work, I can sit home and brood to my heart's content!

Later that afternoon I decide to take a walk through downtown and by whim and whimsy I go into the large antiquarian bookstore on Main Street, reasoning that I might be able to find a used copy of Stephen King's novel, *The Girl Who Loved Tom Gordon*.[1] I read the book when it first came out but since I've become a baseball fan in recent years, and because Tom Gordon is now the Yankees' relief pitcher, I thought it might be fun to read this book again.

The thing is, there's another bookstore in town that specializes in used paperbacks, unlike this one, which is clearly of antiquarian mode rather than modern editions. But my impulse has led me to this place, so what the heck. I walk in the door and the proprietor—a pretty woman about my age, kinda wild red hair, colorful blouse over loden-green slacks—looks up from her reading as I come in, and gives me a lit-tle double-take, which I carefully ignore. The big black Lab behind the counter also looks up, ambles out to say hello, and snogs back to her comfy rug. I like the place already.

I browse the (very interesting) shelves for a while, can't find the King book, and almost leave without saying anything, but instead—one might say impulsively—I go over and ask the woman if she has the title in question. She doesn't, she says, but—if I don't mind her asking—aren't I the author Sue Watkins?

Yow! As always when this happens, I'm taken aback, as if I've been chased out of hiding. Hesitantly, I reply in the affirmative, and brace myself for an onslaught of the usual questions about where Tom Sawyer has gone now that Sam Clemens is dead, or something to that effect. Instead, the woman shuffles through the mess on her desktop and pulls out a copy of *Garden Madness!*[2] My own nine-year-old book!

"I recognized you from your picture," she says, pointing to yet another of my books half-hidden in the pile—*Dreaming Myself*, of all things—which just about knocks me out because that dust-jacket photo was taken eighteen years ago and wow, two books by me right there on her desk! Then she goes on to say that she's given copies of *Garden Madness* to her gardening friends over the years, and they all think it's hilarious.

"What I really like about it is the way you made up words in fake Latin," she adds, and gee I liked that about the book too, though she's the first one who's ever mentioned it, and my ego's beginning to swell up like the *blimpus Goodyearicus*.

Of course I doubt she'd have told me that her friends thought the book was drivel. Nonetheless, Eileen and I end up having a great ranging-over-everything conversation for a couple of hours, very enjoyable, after which she suggests we get together for coffee or lunch at the new Chinese restaurant sometime soon, and I say sure. And the thing is, I mean it. As per my little-thought-tossed-out, she enjoys what I enjoy someone of like mind and reading material (not just by me). Nothing mighty here, no best girlfriends or anything (which I doubt is even possible after the age of fifteen or so, sadly), but an easy, genuine friendship, exactly what I'd envisioned in my fleeting imaginary wish—and contrary to all the hasty codas with which I'd amended it.

I realize that the store I impulsively walked into was a bookstore and not the local plastics factory, so the possibility of finding a bibliocomrade was exponentially enhanced; but the fact is I'd sent out my little thought only an hour or two before walking past the used-paperback store (where I probably would have found a copy of the Stephen King book) and into the antiquarian shop (where I found a new friend).

All very neat.

Next day, I receive an email from Moment Point editor Sue Ray, which says in part: "Not to tease you, but last night I took my first class at the Arnold Arboretum (295 acres of botanical heaven outside of Boston)—Latin Names of Plants. Taught by a charming and brilliant 70-ish word- and garden-obsessed gentleman professor from CUNY (Harvard educated). What fun! I was thinking of you. Tomorrow morning, class #2: Lilac Intensive. Life is good."

In my reply, same day, I describe the whole scene of meeting Eileen (including her specific rave to me about the fake Latin sprinkled through *Garden Madness*), adding this: ". . . and you see the interesting little connection here with you and your gardening-in-the-gardening-heaven class; branching out, so to speak, from the same-old same-old, as I was. And, while this isn't exactly a coincidence, it's kinda charming.

"All very interesting with many nuances, including the fact that in April I made my last garden catalog purchase from my old house: a book on the Latin Names of Plants, a subject that has always fascinated me."

Sue replies, "And isn't it great when a little request—as in, Gee, it would be nice to meet a few like-minded people—is almost instantly answered."

Reading this email exchange (my old marbles glinting in their jar), I thought, yes, little requests answered on command, almost without your having to tag along. And how often coincidences are precognitive in that same specific way, following imagination, which is itself precognitive, or self-fulfilling, or both (these might be the same function).[3] Or how coincidence clusters seem to demonstrate an underlayment of cooperation. The mechanics of telepathy, if you will.

Something else came to me as I wrote back to Sue, so I added this: "Another element of the thing with *The Girl Who Loved Tom Gordon* is that the story revolves around a child who gets lost in the woods and manages to survive because her mother had taught her the names of, and how to recognize, edible plants such as fiddlehead ferns and some New England thing called 'chuckleberries.'

"So here you are telling me this morning that on the same day I met my new friend, you took a class in plant identification in Boston (not only in New England, but in the town where Gordon was a pitcher in the book's timeline). In the story, Tom Gordon appears to the girl in her imagination, then in her dreams, then as a hallucination—or maybe he's actually there, in discorporeal form. But it's the girl's idea of him that saves her life.

"It's really a great book, one of King's best. He doesn't explain or resolve what the girl's vision of Tom Gordon might be, though the implication is that it's some combination of her imaginative abilities, her survival instincts, and the goodness of Tom Gordon himself that does the job. (Her thoughts-tossed-out, as it were.) Interesting that this is the specific book I was looking for when I went into the antiquarian shop. Something more seems to be going on here, though I'm not sure what it is . . . that sense that the coincidence isn't 'finished' yet, that there are more connections forming somewhere beneath the verge.

"Oh well, whatever! Fun!"

Fun, indeed. I was right about coincidences reappearing as unfinished business—as I'd noticed before, much to my amazement.

The Continuing Tale of the Cat on a Leash
How Coincidence Updates Itself

Driving home from Watkins Glen one April afternoon in 1997, an image comes into my mind, for no particular reason, of a woman I'll call Sharon Royce, who lives on the next road north of mine; her house is visible across the open field that lies between. Sharon collects annually for the local cancer fund. I don't know her other than that, and have no other contact with her, beyond running into her occasionally in the P&C grocery; nor do I have any association with the American Cancer Society.

I'm not even going to drive past her house today, so the thought about her seems to be perfectly random. It centers on a conversation I had with her about a year ago, the last time she came to my house collecting for the fund. In that conversation, I'd mentioned seeing her cat one day while I was walking the five-mile square around our roads with Zippy, my Welsh terrier. The cat was wearing a halter leashed to a slide-hook on a clothesline so it could dash back and forth in the yard but not go in the road, a setup normally associated with dogs. I hadn't known whose house it was at the time of my walk, but when Sharon came to my door in 1996, she'd told me where she lived, and I'd said something like, oh yes, the house with the cat on a leash, and she'd explained that this was the only way she'd let her cat go outdoors after another cat of hers had been killed by a car. I ended up giving her all the cash I had on hand, about six dollars, just because of her friendly demeanor and the whole thing about the cat.

In my reverie on this pleasant afternoon in 1997, I'm thinking mostly about the cat, and how funny it was, rushing toward us and yowling at Zippy and me the same way a watchdog might do; and I'm groping through my memory banks trying to remember if it was a Siamese (it seems to be, in my memory; but then again, maybe it isn't). Other than the fund-raising thing, Sharon and I have no social relationship, though she always addresses me as if we were old friends. Moreover, I have little interest in charities and have always been greatly annoyed by sales types soliciting for any reason, and so in every other case except when Sharon shows up, I say no thanks and shut the door.

So anyway, as I'm driving up my road toward home, thinking about Sharon's cat-on-a-leash, I happen to recall a remark she'd made during that 1996 doorway conversation about a young man—was it her own son?—who'd died? Was it of cancer? How? I remember that at the time, I'd been too abashed to ask her for the details, since she clearly assumed I would know who, and what, she was talking about, though I didn't. All of this occupies my mind until I pull into my garage, and then I forget about it.

I'm frazzled by a day full of errands and appointments, so I decide to take Zippy right out for a walk. At nearly 5 P.M. it's still nice outside and we both need the exercise. I don't even take the time to go farther into the house than the garage-level laundry room where Zippy stays while I'm out. I just open the door, snap on his leash, and off we go, all the way back down to the end of the road, a mile or so, and then instead of turning around and walking right back up, we make a long loop across a grass field (an old airport runway, actually), adding at least another mile to our ramble. It's an impulsive and somewhat inconvenient decision on my part to do this, as the runway is lumpy and squishy with late snowmelt. Both the dog and I are going to end up with exceedingly muddy paws before we're done.

Just as we step out from the runway, a car comes down the road, pulls up next to us and stops, and holy moly, who do you think it is but Sharon Royce, and her daughter, out collecting for the Cancer Society (as Sharon leans out the window to tell me)! She says they stopped at my house an hour or so ago and left a collection envelope stuck in my back door. I'm rendered speechless, the details of this coincidence booming through my brain like fireworks, but before I can say anything, Sharon proceeds to tell me, in her friendly, gregarious way, that the local salt mining company is about to be sold and her husband might lose his job after being there for more than twenty-five years, and he's having a really hard time with it.[1]

As she takes a breath, I jump in to tell her how I was thinking about her and her cat no more than an hour ago, but she takes no notice— really, why should she—and continues to relate her quite formidable personal troubles, in the midst of which she makes a reference to the dead boy again—apparently it is her son, or so I gather now—and in an aside gives her daughter a surprisingly accurate rundown on my history as local reporter and the books I've written, and how does she know all this? As usual in our encounters, I'm mystified and embarrassed by the feeling that she knows me well from somewhere (but where?) and that she assumes I know more about her own background than I actually do (but should?).

Eventually she says good-bye and drives on, and I walk straight home and write all of this up longhand, sticking the pages into my dream notebook for later typing and reference. Then I retrieve the charity envelope from the back door and put twenty dollars in it to mail to Sharon in the morning. Even without appearing on my door-step, she has managed to touch my heart (and wallet).

As I think about all this, it seems probable that the random thought that popped into my head about Sharon must have risen out of associations in the back of my mind with the season and my encounter with her the previous year; maybe I'd also read something in the local papers about Cancer Society canvassing, and forgotten it. Several neat and emotionally significant connections here, nonetheless, all depending on specific actions that had to take place to bring this "chance" meeting about.

For one thing, there is the witty little element of my dog being with me on a leash, preceded by my specific recollections of Sharon's cat on a leash (originally observed while walking Zippy, on a leash). For another, if Sharon had gone out on her charity rounds earlier, not only wouldn't I have been home, I wouldn't have met her while walking, either. She'd stuck the collection envelope in a door I rarely used, and who knows how many days would have passed before I found it? Even more precisely, if Zippy and I had simply walked to the end of the road and back without making the detour down the runway, we most likely would have made it home before Sharon drove past us.

Did I, in my casual musings, communicate with Sharon somehow, "arrange" a face-to-face meeting, which led each of us to make adjustments in our plans (such as mine to walk the dog, hers to drive down the road at that particular time) so we could "accidentally" meet? And if so, why? What difference did any of it make to either of us? I didn't think to ask Sharon if she always collected on the same date every year, but even so—is there an element of psychological import for each of us in these annual friendly meetings, not consciously apparent or even explainable in our everyday lives, that we seek out, overcoming the minor obstacles of circumstance to do so? Did it, I mused halfheartedly, have something to do with the fate of this son she kept mentioning, who died in some way I've never understood?

Maybe, I thought, the "charity" here was more on my part, the listening part, than I might suppose. And what, then, for me? A gift from Sharon, making an "inroad," so to speak, on my impatient isolation? Something like that, but elusive, rather the same as Sharon's assumptive camaraderie. And it all seemed centered on the arresting sight of her cat tied out on a leash. A puzzlement!

Months went by, and I didn't think about the Sharon Royce thing again. Then the opening day of deer season came around in November. As usual, it put me in a wretched mood. I posted my fourteen acres of woods and fields, but the morning of deer season's first day is always a fusillade of shotgun blasts from surrounding properties and trucks full of hunters driving up and down the road, deer running frantically everywhere, and I detested the whole thing. I didn't even dare retrieve my morning newspaper out of its roadside box until afternoon, and even then, I would drive or wear a bright orange raincoat to go down and get it.

So here I am sitting at my desk this bleak morning, petulant and glum, slurping coffee and trying not to hear the gunshots peppering the fall air, and on impulse, for distraction's sake if nothing else, I start reading through my 1997 dream notebook. Almost immediately I come across my notes—still untyped—from last April, about Sharon Royce and her cat on a leash, and the little coincidence of our meeting along the road. I'm taken by this all over again, especially the memory of her cat and her (to me) cryptic remarks about her dead boy, and the elusive quality of our acquaintanceship that I can never quite decipher. I make some more notes about it, type up the originals, and pass the time musing about all this until about 9 A.M., when I hear a sudden loud knock on the first-floor sliding glass doors.

I get up, put on my bathrobe—I haven't even gotten out of my pajamas yet—and go downstairs, and who should be standing outside the doors but Sharon Royce!

"Whaddya know!" I say aloud, a little jolt of wow! going through me, and I open the doors to greet her. To my dismay, Sharon explains in her usual friendly tone that she's come to my house this morning because her son wounded a deer on their property and they think it ran across the field and into my woods, and she's asking my permission for him to go in there and look for it.

I'm immediately enraged by this, so much so that my throat closes and I can't reply. After a moment in which we stand there staring at one another, Sharon adds that her son is an excellent hunter and doesn't want to abandon a wounded deer, and because Sharon knows me, he'd asked her to come to my door in his stead, hoping to reassure me of his honest intentions.

I'm not reassured at all. I'm furious on behalf of the wounded and suffering deer, and about the whole notion of hunting to begin with, and am tempted to say no, let the deer die in the soft pines where it belongs, away from the likes of "excellent" hunters such as you. But listening to Sharon, and seeing her honest face, and connecting I suppose with something behind that, something about mothers and sons (and her other lost boy) and I don't know what all, besides the fact that she and I are neighbors and have a history of asking and giving—instead of telling her to go away, I say all right, let him go in and find the deer but please be quick about it, and Sharon says okay, thank you, and I close the door and sit down on the sofa and cry.

Then I go back up to my workroom and read over my notes yet again about the meeting with Sharon on the road, and her mention back then of the apparently dead son; and here she is at my door today—the same day I'd come across these notes for the first time since last April—on behalf of another son and a soon-to-be-dead deer. And there's the aspect of her demeanor winning out over my repugnance for hunting, parallel to the way her demeanor always wins over my dislike of door-to-door sales, as well as my reservations about charities, especially medical charities.

Mixed in here, it occurs to me, is the fact that Sharon comes to my door on behalf of a charity that is ostensibly trying to stop a disease that kills; today she's here on behalf of a ritual whose purpose (whatever the arguments for it) is killing. Moreover she appeared on my doorstep in the exact moment I'd been reading about our previous encounter—which was itself a connection with a previous encounter, all hinged together by my thoughts about animals. None of the animals in question today had been on a leash, though certainly all of them are hemmed in by human beliefs and stupidity, I muse gloomily.

What was going on? There was something in all of this about official ideas of both disease (fight it with money) and animals (fight their alleged overpopulation—while ignoring our own—with guns), and in each case, a certain factor of economics prevailed, as well as the notion of "cutting out" the scourge in question (though both scourges ironically support the industries that seek to eradicate the scourge). And all of it defined by chance conversations with a person I instinctively liked—who would probably say that accidents and disease were "chance," though in a different context from the one I meant—and with whom I'd felt an underlying affiliation from the beginning. Why? What did all this mean?

Or was there even a meaning to be discerned, in that regard? What if all this represented an accumulation of example in some fashion; an illustration-puzzle meant to focus my attention on something important? Important for Sharon, too, therefore. I could guess at some of it, but it was all couched in layers of metaphor and supposition.

Not long after this, I found out through my hairdresser that Sharon had indeed lost a son, in 1986, in a car crash not far from his home. It had been in all the papers, though in the midst of moving that same year, I'd somehow missed it. Well, there was one eerie and awful tendril with the cat on the leash, kept tied up so it wouldn't die in the road (as the other cat had also). That image, of the cat, was the little random memory that had started these coincidence-associations, and as I listened to my hairdresser describe the accident, I felt deep chagrin for my anger with Sharon about the deer (though I was unapologetic about my grief).

And the circle of coincidence wasn't done with us yet.

Six years later, while combing through my records in preparation for this book, I come across my notes once again about Sharon Royce, and how it was that in 1997, the previous time I read over my notes about her, she'd come to my door the same day, about the wounded deer. How odd—how strangely prescient, almost—that I'd run into her in the P&C just a few days before this current note-reading. She'd greeted me in her usual friendly way, but I hadn't recognized her at first, and then realized it had been quite a while since I'd seen her, at least a couple of years. Was she no longer collecting for the Cancer Society? I didn't have a chance to ask, because she was with an elderly, meticulously groomed gentleman who was obviously confused, and kept trying to wander off, taking up most of her attention. Was it her father, grandfather? She didn't explain, just took his arm and steered him gently down the grocery aisle. "See you sometime," she'd called back to me, cheerful as always.

Again, that mysterious state of my never quite knowing what I felt I ought to know about Sharon's life. Exactly like the long tale of her cat, and this odd connection Sharon and I seem to keep refreshing, and what is it, exactly, that sets this into motion? I study all this, jot a few marginal remarks about coincidence seeming to update itself in ways than appear to be outside the measure of happenstance. Such as me looking over my notes about Sharon and then Sharon coming to my door in almost the same moments as my reading about her. As if we call out to one another on levels other than, say, just calling one another up on the phone (which we never did). I must use this in *What a Coincidence!* But how?

So here I am, reading my notes, trying to suss out some kind of format for this book. Sometimes the ongoing thread of coincidences baffles me. Such events seem to occur in units, rather than linear time. We perceive them in time because that's how we perceive reality, but it isn't the way they happen. Coincidence is "fat." Rather, coincidental events have a *thickness* to them that even allowing for the sharpshooter effect suggests a simultaneous nature of past, present, and future. Intuitively, we recognize this, even in the dumbest of conspiracy theories.

There's an inner order to coincidence, of that I'm certain; but what it is, or how to demonstrate it, seems to reside at the far edge of my capacity to explain. Possibly this isn't what you'd call a failing; it could be a reflection of the intellect's abilities in general, as they seek to evolve. It's also quite possible that I'm full of shit. Whatever, I'm on my own here, or so it seems.

Feeling a bit discouraged, I get up from my desk and take a walk around the snowy February yard and down to the mailbox. Among the other items inside it is a copy of Cat Fancy magazine, with a picture of rag doll cats (Siamese with white toes) on the cover. I don't subscribe to Cat Fancy, but since I bought a cat-hotel gizmo online a while ago for Sean's fat old Siamese, Chauncey, I immediately assume that this magazine is a promotional issue sent out in response to that purchase.

The rag doll cats also remind me of a very peculiar white-toed Siamese kitten that my friend Barbara Coultry and I bought in 1966 from a Syracuse pet shop while we were college roommates. Almond was a major pill, is what he was, but loveable all the same. Eventually Barbara took him home with her, and he'd been an energetic center of her parents' adoration for many years. Unfortunately, Barbara's husband and son suffer from extreme allergies, so she can no longer have a cat, and she has often mentioned how much she misses them. It occurs to me, remembering Almond, that Barbara would enjoy the magazine, so after looking through it briefly, I stick it in a manila envelope and set it out in the next morning's mail.

According to an email from her, Barbara received the magazine that Saturday. On Sunday, she emailed this: "Someone named Sharon Royce who lives on _____ Road is probably going to end up wondering why she never got her March issue of Cat Fancy. Maybe I should send it to her without any explanation whatsoever other than that the mail delivery person must have had a bad day. She'll look at the postmark on the envelope that mentions Rensselaer, New York, and wonder about this postman/woman."

Stunned, I read Barbara's email again. Holy Toledo! That magazine belonged to *Sharon Royce*? I hadn't bothered to look at the address
label after jumping to the conclusion that it was a promotional sample
(connected with Sean's Siamese cat), meant for me. And that same
morning—once again!—I'd been reading over my notes about the
whole coincidence cluster with Sharon Royce, which had all started
with my notice of her cat on a leash! Had it been a Siamese or not?
Again, I try to remember—it had certainly yowled like a Siamese, but I
just can't recall for sure. And that particular issue of *Cat Fancy* had on
its cover a type of cat breed that looked, to my eye anyway, like a
Siamese knock-off, marked like the Siamese kitten Barbara and I had
bought from that pet shop so many years ago.

Once more, then, into the question: Had I unconsciously set up
this little "event" in the Sharon Royce series by purposefully not seeing
her name on the magazine's address label? Had I seen it, I would have
left it in the mailbox for redelivery, though the connection with reading
my cat-specific Sharon notes would have been interesting nonetheless.
But since I didn't, at least consciously, realize the magazine was mis-
delivered, sending it to Barbara added another dimension to it all. How
did she fit into this loop? If there was a loop in the first place.

Well, it happens that Barbara had been going through a miserable time, across many months of unrelenting complications, trying to
manage care for her increasingly incapacitated and difficult mother.
Which made me think of Sharon's allusions to her own difficult life,
the elderly fellow in her care that day in the supermarket, and the genuinely good-hearted soul that she is, a quality that had touched me in
moments when with anyone else I might have been thoughtless or
downright rude. Just reading my notes about her set off a connection
frenzy every time—but how? And why? It had all started with me
thinking about her cat, way back in 1997, "for no particular reason."
Now it seemed to be concluding with a cat—not on a leash, but in
a magazine.

Maybe there was something in here for the three of us, some helpful attitude-sharing or coincidence-swap involving characteristic ways of handling situations. A pretty far-out notion, I had to concede, though it felt right, or hinted at the right direction. Hints also, of the spacious present, of how events expand beneath the surface of daily life, rather than merely clunk along from one thing to the next. Hints of the conscious mind's capacity to gather up associations and connections best suited to our underlying well-being. And to keep bringing these to our attention until we caught on, maybe. Now there was an idea to chew on: Coincidence updates as indicator of benevolent morality play.

Barbara did return the magazine to Sharon with a funny little note explaining the mix-up. In a later email, Barbara wrote, "I got [post] mail from Sharon Royce, and after reading it and seeing how touched and pleased she was that I went through the trouble and expense of mailing her the magazine, I'm really glad I did it. I got the feeling she wasn't used to people being honest and taking the time for small kindnesses."

Ouch, I thought, reading this email: There it is, or at least some of it. In all the years I lived across that big, empty field from Sharon, I never once went over to pay her a visit, or visited anyone else who lived around there for that matter. A comment, perhaps, on the downside of aloofness, and the remedies hidden in simple (or maybe not so simple) acts of charity that we can all give and receive? And weaving in and around this idea was a set of recurring coincidences that moved through time, with appropriate updates and use of recognizable thematic threads, exactly the way recurring dreams appear. Until we get it? Until we catch the point being made? Our own consciousness nudging itself? Toward what, do you suppose?

9

Didn't Do X, Which Leads to Y
Impulse and the Coincidence of Not

So you'd think that after all this time and concentration on random thoughts, impulses, and coincidental outcomes I'd recognize my intuitions at work, and follow through on them automatically, just do what they say every time, without question. Well, of course I don't. Who does? Our thought process is made up of many different elements, some familiar and some not so much so, but all are meant to be used in concert, and in context. Using dream information to fill out your income tax form is probably not a good idea, for instance. And we're set up to know the difference. It's when we divide our psyche into rigid categories and insist that only some are "real" that we get into trouble, or lose out on the fullness of consciousness.

The discomfiting thing about the idea that coincidence may be demonstrating that fullness is that it treads on the safe boundaries we make around the divisions. Even when an impulse to do something is completely benign (take the card to the post office, walk around the runway), we tend to haggle with it, as if it could con us into doing something awful against our will. Amusingly, we haggle just as much over impulses to *not* do something, as if not-doing is the eighth deadly sin, tempting us to shirk our duties. Hunches collide with habit and obligation. We shouldn't! We should! I don't feel like it! Do it! It's as if we need to find coincidence waiting on the other side, as much for reassurance as the wow.

Take, for example, the following didn't-do tale.

DIDN'T CALL RACHAEL

June 2003: I make a note to myself to call Rachael at the Dundee Fabric Shop about one of the sewing projects I took to her some weeks ago. Along with two quilts that needed repair was a woolen square with my great-great grandmother's embroidered initials and the date, 1833, that I'd cut out of a moth-eaten blanket. Originally I'd asked Rachael to make a pillow out of this square, but now I wish I hadn't taken it to the shop for that; what I really want to do is frame it. The pillow is going to be expensive, for one thing, and the wool fabric is so old that it probably won't hold up very long under that sort of use.

But even though I keep looking at my note to call and cancel this project, I keep not following through. Either I forget about it thirty seconds after I look at the note, or I'm so filled with ennui at the idea of calling the shop that I just never get around to doing so, even though I don't want to have the pillow made anymore.

A day or two later, Rachael calls to tell me that my items are done, and I go into Dundee to pick them up, and discover that she forgot to do anything at all with the woolen square! She's mortified, but I assure her it's okay, I'd changed my mind anyway, it all worked out! Now I can frame the piece and hang it up, if I ever get around to *that.*

Did my change of mind about the pillow communicate itself to Rachael? Or did I pick up on her forgetting to do the pillow, which I'd interpreted as not needing to make the phone call to cancel that job? Or both? Whichever, it's pretty neat.

Then there's the interesting didn't-do of suddenly not wanting to bother with a pleasant routine for no reason you can consciously discern—until the "reason" bubbles up in canny coincidental foresight:

DIDN'T WRITE DOWN THE DREAM

I have a vivid and lengthy dream in July 2004 that I don't bother to write down. Somehow I just can't drum up the slightest enthusiasm for recording the thing. I jot some quick notes about the dream and set them aside, highly unusual for me, and forget about it until way into September, when I find my notes in the mess on my desk and decide to type them up, finally. I'd recorded plenty of dreams between then and now, so why I'd felt this lead-weight non-caring don't-wanna about this one from July is a mystery.

Among other things, the dream focused on a woman leading a beautiful white llama on a rope leash along a path. I'm supposed to take photos of all the figures in this dream, including the llama, so I walk up close to it, and its sweet, lovely white face fills my dream-camera frame. It turns out the woman wants to write a biography of Al S., a friend of mine from Dundee who died in 1999. I wonder if I can help her with the details. As I contemplate this, I'm suddenly walking along Main Street in the village where I now live. The sidewalk is very clear.

Many other details here, but the interesting thing is that as I sit at my desk to type up this dream—nearly two months after dreaming it—I happen to look out my workroom window and see Joan, the town library's historian, walking along the sidewalk with her two West Highland terriers. I should add here that I rearranged my workroom just days before this, so my desk faces the big front window, or I probably wouldn't have noticed her walking by at all. We've chatted before while she walks these jaunty dogs, but today I notice that she's carrying one of them in her arms. Concerned, I jump up and dash out the door to ask if the dog is okay.

Turns out it's the older doggie, who's just tired. As Joan and I talk, she happens to mention that the local historical society has been collecting house histories, and they've been stuck trying to find out more information about a particular house in Dundee. To my surprise, as Joan describes it, I realize it's the house where Al and his wife were living at the time of his death! Moreover, I'd researched and written up a history of that house back in the seventies (before Al's family owned it) for a news-paper project—so as it turns out, I can indeed help her with "the details."

Among other subtle connections with my dream, it's notable that Westies have silky white fur, and a visage not unlike a llama's, and that I was standing right up close to this dog's sweet face as Joan and I spoke. Plus, she was leading the two of them on a single long rope leash, very cute.

None of these coincidental elements—including the historical society benefiting from my house research—would have come about if I'd written the dream down at the time that I dreamed it. Instead, I put it off for two months and then sat down to write it on the exact day, and in the exact moment, when I would see Joan walk by my window with her dogs, jump up impulsively to go out on the sidewalk to talk with her, and make these evocative connections with this specific dream, and no other.

Inconsequential examples, really—you do something, or you don't do something, against all logic, and the result surprises you with almost magical resolve. Of course there are those times you think you know exactly what you're doing (or not doing) and it ends up in a mess. Could it be you were acting in disconnect from your own intuitions, refusing to acknowledge their signals? Or is every decision a lottery draw in the face of chance, a leap into the unknowable, no matter what kind of information we base it on? And yet it seems to me that the idea of "chance" and the "unknown" (which have their own beauty in a larger sense) is based on the assumption that the precognitive elements of intuition and coincidence are flukes rather than natural components of the conscious mind.

As in . . .

Didn't Resist the French Fries

A nice fall day in 2004, except that my computer's been acting up lately and I have an appointment with the fix-it shop in Watkins Glen, which is a long drive from where I live now. So off I go to use up most of a day on behalf of my writing machine. By the time they've solved the problem and I do a couple more errands, the light breakfast I ate this morning has run its course and I'm hungry. There are plenty of good restaurants in town, but for some reason I decide that all I want are French fries from the local Burger King.

It's ridiculous—I just want to go home! Don't I? No, I'm seized with this (for sweet-tooth me, unusual) craving, and moreover I realize I have the urge to go through the drive-around window, something I haven't done on my own in so long I can't even remember it—literally, maybe fifteen years. I hate sitting in line chugging car exhaust into the atmosphere; hate the indignity of ordering food from a machine; hate the idea of being served by hands that have been touching money and take-out window countertops and cash register buttons and who knows what else—but there it is, a big stupid impulse to go through take-out and get some hot, greasy French fries and a diet pop for lunch.

Well, there is logic and wisdom and then there is the intrigue of impulses. I decide to follow this one, with reservations. First I drive past Burger King to check the take-out line, and it looks as though there are only two cars in it, so I think, okay, why not? So I pull in their driveway, and the minute I get around behind the parking lot I see there are actually five or six cars ahead of me, which were hidden from the street angle, and I can't back out because two more cars have come right in behind me, and there I am, stuck and embarrassed. What if somebody I know sees me here?

Furthermore, the line is insanely slow and it takes almost forty-five minutes to get to the window and pick up the goddamned fries and diet soda and get OUT of there and on my way home. Forty-five minutes! What in the hell was that impulse about? I don't need the calories, I don't need to waste the gas; I could have gone home and had something decent for lunch and it would have worked out to not a whole lot more time spent hungry, either. Impulses! Bah!

Still, those fries smell awfully good, and so I drive out of town and into the countryside, munching and slurping—and about ten miles outside the village I come around a bend in the road, and the highway up ahead is completely blocked off by a huge knot of emergency vehicles, lights flashing everywhere. Plainly, there has been some sort of massive accident. According to the volunteer fireman who is detouring traffic onto a side-road, it happened about half an hour or forty-five minutes ago (I open my window and ask him this).

Later, I found out that a mail route carrier had stopped on the highway to make a left turn and a tractor-trailer truck had come up over the rise behind her and plowed into the back of her car, smashing both vehicles to pieces and spewing gasoline everywhere. The woman was taken to an Elmira hospital in critical condition and the truck driver was treated for minor injuries.[1] How awful, how random. Or so it must be, isn't it? But as I turn off onto the side road, the thought that fills my mind is that if I hadn't followed my impulse and ended up stuck in that takeout line at BK, I might very well have been right in the middle of this collision. The timing is certainly right and, moreover, the feeling I have about it is quite intense. My legs are weak and rubbery, and I realize I'm panting, as if I've been running rather than sitting behind the wheel.

It reminds me of the time I'd been waiting to exit a parking lot in Watkins Glen and the driver of a car coming down the street toward me turned her right-side signal on, as if to enter the lot, meaning that I could pull out and go on, which I started to do. But suddenly I'd heard my late father's voice in my head, as plainly as if he were sitting beside me, teaching me how to drive all those years ago, barking the command (as he frequently did), "Never trust anybody!" Loud and clear and so poignantly real that I put on the brake, and the woman sailed right past me, not turning in at all. Had I pulled out, which her signal clearly indicated I could do, she would have T-boned my driver's side door.

So what is this about? Are impulses and coincidence the physical conduit of precognition? Clairvoyance the voice of our own precognitive abilities? Maybe, I think as I drive along the country road that will eventually lead me back to the highway and home, it's that impulses work in what we think of as a linear fashion and coincidence is more sideways, or multi-layered; but that both, or all these facilities—the recognition of coincidence, precognition, clairvoyance, telepathy—are aspects of the conscious mind at work as it accesses its own knowledge; words we use to identify inherent capabilities we only dimly understand. After all, how does the finite mind (meaning the portion of consciousness focused so thoroughly in physical reality) comprehend the infinite (or however far the mind's abilities can reach, and why would there be any limits at all if it can access even a portion of what I suspected it could)?

Maybe the only way to grasp the infinite really is to know the self (the personal as universal)—or at least catch a glimpse of what's possible by following coincidence trails and precognitive information whenever you can for however far you can manage it. Hints, anyway, of how Things Might Work.

Of course no one knows how many accidents we avoid without any conscious recognition of having done so;[2] and there are times when nothing saves you, or when for some unknown reason your impulses and ordinary decisions take you into the path of harm, as in the case of the mail carrier's car that "just happened" to be in the wrong place at the wrong time. Can you say with equal enthusiasm, then, that this is the result of the power of the conscious mind? And yet it is, though such outcomes would involve layers of intent (if you're going to consider events in that light) that could only be dissected by the people involved, if at all.

Rationalization on my part, maybe; or survivor's guilt, or something like it—I did feel somewhat euphoric, driving along, as if I'd been given a second chance by my own wiles. Which was silly, really, since if I'd left town without stopping for eats I could have just as easily missed the accident scene altogether. I'd never know for sure. All I had were the funny little intuitive jabs I was getting about it, and the equally unset-tling idea that if you really did stop to analyze every single little impulse and coincidence-meaning and bit of intuitive information (maybe even your ennui) that you thought you were picking up, you'd probably never leave the house or do anything of even remote uncertainty, and what fun would life be then?

Or, maybe this warning system (including voices from dead rela-tives) has been part of our consciousness from the beginning, when our ancestors roamed a world lit only by the stars, and we can rely on that system's inherent design without needing to analyze it ad nauseum—unless we're interested in discovering what it is, exactly, that our con-sciousness is capable of in the first place.

Meanwhile, it seems that even greasy fast food can turn out to be good for you once in a while.[3] And leading from that, here's a type of didn't-do impulse-following on another scale, probably meaningless in itself—or else it has import of such mind-bending importance that even I can't put it into words:

DIDN'T BUY THE IODINE TABLETS

Somewhere not long after 9/11: Old nightmares and anxieties from growing up in the Cold War era have resurfaced lately, for obvious rea-sons. I thought all that was over with, and now look what we've come to, again. I'm sure this sentiment has occurred to everybody who glued themselves to the TV throughout that terrible time.

In the midst of this, as if 9/11 weren't bad enough, tensions between Pakistan and India escalate and the sound of bristling nuclear weapons is once again heard in the world. Surfing the Net one after-noon, I hit on a website extolling potassium iodine tablets as protection against the radioactive cloud that will encircle the earth should these two countries let fly their missiles.

Suddenly, it's as if every bomb shelter plan, every scenario from the sixties I ever imagined about nuclear war, has reincarnated in front of my eyes. These tablets seem the wisest thing anybody could have. I'm going to buy a pack for me and a pack for my dog. Maybe I'll buy a couple packs to keep in the car. To have while Zippy and I are fleeing the death cloud, of course.

As I go through the steps necessary to purchase these tablets, it seems that with every click of the mouse, my certainty that this disaster is going to happen ratchets up another notch. By the time I get to the last link, one more click and the deal is sealed, I'm ready to grab Zippy and start living in the closet under the staircase right now, because it's going to happen any minute, and we're all going to suffer from it horribly for years on end. It's only smart to get these tablets now, before it's too late. Anyone would say so.

My finger hovers.

Then something comes to me, something like a burst of anger. I sit back in my chair. NO, dammit, I think—*I am not going to bank on that future.* I am not going to buy those tablets. I'm not going to buy that outcome! Instead I'm going to bank on the future in which Pakistan and India back off, and work to resolve their differences. I'll risk it. I'll take the chance. I'll dare to think it matters what I do about it, here all alone, just me and the mouse.

I disconnect from the website, and go on to something else, and forget all about iodine tablets.

Well, you know what happened—so far, as of this date in 2005, these two countries, at least, have indeed backed away from the nuclear edge and are making some diplomatic headway between them. Of course, the mess in Iraq is escalating by the minute, and fanatics exist in every country as we've all seen too well, but that's not what this was about—if this little "didn't do" is "about" anything. And it's not that I think my not-buying decision caused distant minds to change. No, the mind that changed here was my own, a fork in my personal world's road.

As if your imaginative abilities can lead you through the dark. As if you can live anywhere, in whatever world you believe is possible.

10

Lies I Apparently Didn't Tell
The Blatantly-Making-It-Up Coincidence

Scott and Laura, my house buyers, have been reassuring me about the birds. I was as attached to the many varieties of songbirds that came to the numerous feeders I hung all around that house as anything else about it. When I moved, I left the feeders and supplies behind, hoping the new owners would take up the hobby, which they have. Today, Laura sent me a particularly nice email, telling me not to worry about my feathered friends, as she and Scott have come to love watching the mix of songbirds, squirrels, chipmunks, rabbits, and other forest denizens eating their fill outside the windows.

I'm overjoyed by this, that the people who bought my house like the same things about it that I did, and in an effusive gush of gratitude, I email a thank you to Laura in which I tell her about the birds around my friend Dave's rural home, which has a slightly different ecosystem than exists around my old place. "We've watched orioles build a nest and fledge three babies," I write to her, "heard a black-billed cuckoo in the swamp, watched turkey vultures eat road kill, and generally had some thrilling bird days." I tap out some additional words of bird-lore, and am about to hit the "send" button . . . but sit there staring at the screen instead.

Why did I write that?

Sure, there are oriole babies in the tree by Dave's house, and yeah, we've heard the cuckoo, and there are lots of other interesting birds, including pileated woodpeckers and a cock pheasant strolling through the yard, all very report-worthy. But the thing is, though we're enthusiastic birders and have often observed turkey vultures soaring overhead, we've never seen one eating road kill anywhere, let alone near the house. Turkey vultures are relatively shy birds for all their size and reputation, and if I had seen such a sight as the one I just described, I would have been totally awestruck. But no—I made it up!

Well, it's a good story, and as I was writing it I could see the vulture clearly in my mind, sitting on a hunk of road kill in the ditch weeds, tearing it to shreds . . . except that it didn't happen. I'm a little ashamed of myself. But then I think, oh what the hell, and I send the email to Laura as is. In for a penny, in for a pound o' rotten flesh.

Next afternoon, Dave and I are sitting in his living room reading newspapers when I look out the picture window and spot a turkey vulture soaring in the sky above the cornfield directly across the road. As we watch, the vulture does something remarkable: it circles lower and lower, lands awkwardly in the grass at the top of the tall, weedy roadside bank, folds its enormous wings, and proceeds to march down the slope until it comes to a dark lump that looks to us like just another rock— until the bird starts pulling it apart! Through binoculars it's plain the unfortunate lump is either a dead squirrel or a mourning dove, which up to this point has been hidden from our notice. Unusually heedless of our presence in the window, the vulture rips and gulps in joyful gourmand splendor. We're just absolutely flabbergasted. Dave grabs his camcorder and films the entire scene. "Can't wait to show the grandkids," he exclaims happily.

So what's going on here? Obviously I'm intensely interested in the habits of birds and moreover have a natural affection for the macabre, whether in nature or storytelling, and vultures are particularly iconic in that regard. Once scarce in this area, turkey vultures have increased their range throughout the northeast over the past couple of decades, so it's not uncommon anymore to see them wheeling overhead, looking for lunch. But this is the first time either of us has ever seen one land on something this close to human activity.[1] Did I clairvoyantly foresee the upcoming vulture feast and incorporate it into my email about bird observations? Or did I make up a story whole cloth that later "came true" in a far more literal expression of "thoughts tossed out" than even I was prepared to accept? Some combination of these elements, an unfolding of imagination and event that we don't ordinarily consider, or even deem possible?

This is tricky stuff. There are words for people who think they're the center of everything ("narcissistic" comes to mind)—and yet, where else does daily experience come from but the individual experiencing it? Picturing a thing and seeing the thing emerge in reality isn't, after all, an entirely radical idea. It's used in such areas as disease recovery, stress relief, even business seminars. But this is something else, something beyond the cause-and-effect of self-hypnotism and good suggestion-giving. While my vulture tale is hardly landscape-transforming (though fiction has acted as portent often enough in history), there are elements in it suggesting a precognitive construction process, a world built on algorithms of imagination and result, with coincidence acting as a staging area for the work in progress.

Taking this making-it-up equation a cautious step further, here's one involving a warning I left behind for Scott and Laura: The deck on that house is accessible by three sets of sliding-glass doors and one solid door. All of them have locks, but the wooden door has an odd two-stage deadbolt that tricked me one cold winter night when I stepped out on the deck in bathrobe and slippers to toss chicken bones into the yard (*something* always ate the leftovers) and the door snicked shut behind me. Suddenly I was locked out of the house, temperature about five above zero, all other doors shut and locked, no outdoor key, no way to get in. I was home alone, the nearest neighbor a mile's wade up the snow-filled road and my feet already turning numb.

Trying not to panic, thinking there just had to be some way to get back inside, I clambered over the deck rail into the knee-deep snow below and slogged around the house checking windows in last-hope desperation; and by a wild stroke of incredible luck I discovered that for unknown reasons of stupidity or prescience I'd left the first-floor bathroom window ajar just enough that I could get my rapidly-freezing fingers inside it, pry the thing open, and squiggle inside. I was blue with cold, soaked with snow, bruised from the break-in, and the window hinge would need to be repaired, but I was going to live to tell about it.

Or at least this is the story I write up for Scott and Laura as part of an information packet I put together for them. They're coming from California and don't know about winter "house tricks," as I call that one. As I look it over I'm a little embarrassed by the zeal with which I've told this locked-out tale. In fact, it comes to me that I might have made some of it up. But I'm no longer sure how much of it is fiction and how much of it is true.

I know I was locked out, and I clearly remember how I climbed over the deck rail and waded through the snow (didn't I?), but how I got back in the house . . . well, how did I "really" get back in the house? Now I can't remember if the way I wrote it is the way it happened or not! I must have pried the bathroom window open—how else could I get back in? That house is a fortress, every door and window secure; the only weak link would be if I'd left something open, which I sort of remembering doing . . . to vent steam from the shower, right? Or did I? No matter how hard I try to recall what I "actually" did, it slips away like a shadow, leaving only my story as I've written it. But I did lock myself out, and I did climb over the railing—I'm not inventing this. Am I? Did *any* of it happen? I can no longer tell!

Well, there's a clue to memory reconstruction, all right. Next thing you know I'll recall seeing Sasquatch out in the woods (maybe he's the one eating the chicken bones). But whatever its origins, the door-lock caveat is a good one, so I leave the story as is and go on about my packing.

Scott and Laura moved in on the weekend of May 1. According to an email from Laura, Scott went out on the deck just after midnight a few nights later to have a smoke, the door slipped shut behind him, and there he was, locked out! No snow on the ground, but it was a cold, damp night, and Scott was wearing only light pajamas and slippers. Sleeping soundly, Laura didn't hear his frantic pounding on the deck doors. Even the dog just stood there staring at him through the glass, no help at all.

Finally, Scott crawled over the railing and walked around the house, pounding on the other doors and windows, to no avail. He ended up huddled in the garage (which they'd fortunately left open) in a nest of mover's blankets until 3:30 A.M., when Laura woke up, realized Scott wasn't in the house, and went looking for him. "After that," Laura concluded with gentle irony, "was when Scott read your warning about the deck door."

Of course it goes without saying that lots of made-up scenarios never happen—lottery wins (for most of us) spring to mind here, along with daydreams of mayhem, romance, and revenge, to name an obvious few. Still, if we kept consistent track of the pictures that seem to flicker at random through our imaginations, we might be surprised how much of it materializes in synchronistic events both large and small, and what those events demonstrate about what we're actually imagining (as opposed to what we think we're imagining) in the first place. Playfully, I once "knew" I could find fun stuff like marbles and pocket change just by thinking about them in a certain way; later, grown-up me might think I'd like to win a gazillion dollars, but the energy behind that idea isn't the same. My imagination's effectiveness comes with limits on how much money I think is too obscenely much, not to mention my strong aversion to the public exposure involved in lottery hits. Perhaps childishly, I'd rather have the secret little feedbacks, the coincidental finds, the magic mulch, the turkey vulture flying down from the sky as if he'd read my made-up script. I'd rather have the stories, in other words—that's where my true interest lies.

So are these coincidental imagination-mirrors examples of precognition? Of the intricate relationship between expectations and actual experience? Intuitive application of the ever-roaming Google mind? And how often does this "work?" All the time? Sometimes? Depending on what? Is it as simple as the atmosphere in which one does the imagining? Because it's been my experience that rage, desperation, or anxiety seem to shatter this connection between imagination and outcome, almost as if there's a natural safety valve built into our worst fears about such things—as in this example:

It's early September of 2004, and I've hardly slept a wink all night, lying awake in an obsessive froth of worry. A week or so ago, I ripped out the tangle of weeds and half-dead bushes that had choked the garden area along the shady side of my apartment house, then spent another day planting new perennials and spreading many bags of mulch over all. Then I rummaged through some broken marble slabs piled out behind the garage and hauled three or four pieces out for garden stepping-stones and added a few fossil rocks for extra feng shui. The result is quite charming, if I do say so.

But now it's all going to be spoiled. Two days ago, workers started replacing the roof, and the first thing they did was shuck the old shingles off the front section, sending a cascade of debris down on the bushes around the porch, crushing everything. I hadn't realized they were going to do this now, or I'd have waited to plant my little side-garden, which is unscathed so far, but they're coming back in the morning, and I just know they're going to ruin it.

Over and over, I lie there imagining the pile of old shingles and nails crashing down on my pretty plants and rocks. I see this vividly, in bright color and sound. I become so focused on these images that I make myself sick—I have to get up and gulp some Pepto-Bismol, which doesn't help. Hours pass, shingles fall, flowers die, I toss and turn. Finally I resolve to rush out at dawn and dig up all the plants and move everything out of the way, the logical solution. But then I start obsessing about how to get this done before the workers arrive. I imagine infuriating, screeching arguments with them about waiting for me to finish, and this loop plays again and again until I fall into an uneasy twilight doze from which I'm abruptly awakened at 7 A.M. by the sound of the men climbing on the roof! Oh, no! I'm too late! Frantically, I jump up and run outside to scream in my garden's defense.

Except that it turns out they're not even going to work on that side of the roof—the shingles overhanging the little garden are in fine shape. There won't be any debris coming down on it at all. My night's racking anxiety, with its enormously overwrought visualizations of disaster, not to mention one of the worst stomachaches of my life, was for nothing.

But—why didn't this "work?" If ever I sent thoughts out into the universe or imagined something happening in the near future, last night was a supreme example of concentrated storytelling. Yet the opposite of my worst fears was the thing that came true. As I scuttle back inside to make coffee and avoid the startled looks of the workmen—who's this crazed-looking dame in a ratty old bathrobe, anyway?—it occurs to me that whenever I get into one of these anxiety-ridden worry-obsessions (as with my pre-impulse futz over the comic books), it seems that the thing I'm focused on in that state rarely, if ever, happens, and in fact its opposite almost always does.

You'd think if this stuff operates in anything approaching a logical, provable fashion, or even in strictly intuitive terms, then the effort I poured into this picture would have emerged as feared, or worse, and I'd go out there in the morning to find the entire roof lying on the garden with maybe a dead cow on top. But no. Nothing came of it at all! Quite unlike my playful little thoughts-tossed-out or offhand made-up stories with no particular energy or second-guessing behind them one way or the other.[2]

Maybe the matrix of reality doesn't respond as easily to desperation as it does to something positive, in the way that you can't force water and oil to mix. Maybe there's a chemistry, or electrical charge, attached to various states of mind that makes playfulness more naturally compatible with the physical world. If so, it would explain much about the ratio of worst-fears versus best-hopes that seem to operate on a mass level as well as an individual one. For all our herky-jerky history, as a species we've lived up to our best hopes, the optimistic made-up imaginings as it were, about as often as not.

11

How Much Do We Know
and How Do We Know It?

A Glimpse into the Spacious Present

A pretty Sunday, May 23, 1999: Dave and I go to a restaurant in Watkins Glen for dinner. Maybe five minutes after we sit down, who should walk in and sit in the booth behind us but Natalie, an old pal of mine from Dundee days, and her new husband. For some reason the moment I see Natalie, I think about the fact that she appears, nameless, in *Dreaming Myself, Dreaming a Town*, telling me a dream while we're sitting at a booth in a local diner way back in 1979.

The last time I talked with Natalie was about three weeks previous to this, when the four of us had all run into one another in this same restaurant. At that time, Natalie had told me about the death of Ann, a therapist she and I had each consulted briefly in the mid-eighties. Unknown to me, Ann had been dead for three years by then and I had in fact gone over to Natalie's table specifically to ask about Ann, and was very much taken aback by the news. Now on this May evening, Natalie and I greet each other and she says, "I had a dream about you last night."

I turn around in my booth seat and say, "I hope it wasn't too weird."

"Not at all," she says. "It began with you disputing a fact."

"Well, that's true to life," I say, and we both laugh. Turns out the disputed dream-fact is that I didn't believe Ann was really dead. I kept insisting that she wasn't, Natalie says. In her dream, she and I were standing near a place on a sheer cliff overlooking Seneca lake, looking off across the water while we argued. "There were some other details," Natalie says, and then she glances at her husband and adds, "but that's all I'm going to tell you."

Well, dreams can be revealing, all right, so I don't press Natalie about this. Instead, I remind her that about ten years ago, Ann and her husband had moved from Ithaca, New York, to a house on a cliff's edge overlooking Seneca Lake, but sold the place shortly thereafter and moved back to Ithaca because it was so difficult to get in and out of the driveway in winter. Natalie looks quite surprised by this, then says she'd consciously forgotten that Ann and her husband had ever owned a house on Seneca Lake. *Recalling* this fact, as it connects with her dream, has quite an impact on her, which strikes me as similar to her dream's vision of me *disputing* a fact (the fact of Ann's death). A psychological echo between us of some sort?

Also, what Natalie doesn't know is that the day before this, Dave and I had rented a small place on Seneca Lake for the long Memorial Day weekend, and it's located on the edge of a steep wooded hillside, with a paved driveway that falls so precipitously to the narrow shoreline that driving, let alone walking, either up or down it is a challenge and we've already decided we won't rent there again because of this. (We've even exchanged comments about what a nightmare the place would be in winter, if anyone were crazy enough to try living there in the off-season.)

Oddly, to me anyway, when I tell this neat little tie-in to Natalie, it seems to mean nothing at all to her—her own "recalled" memory of Ann's cliffside house is obviously still occupying her thoughts, to the exclusion of any possible connection between her dream and my weekend retreat.

We all turn back to the business of ordering food, but after a few minutes, Natalie says, "You know, Sue," to get my attention and adds, "I found out about Ann's death in a secondhand way too, and quite a while afterward like you did, so maybe that's what my dream was about." Her tone is sympathetic—she also remembers the day she told me about Ann, and my reaction. So I reply with, "Yes, that element of disbelief when you discover that someone has vanished. It's hard to resolve." Which is like the feeling I have about Natalie's dream—that it's more important than it appears. But why is that? I don't know. At this point our respective meals show up and that's the end of it for this night.

The next afternoon, Monday, Dave and I vacate the cliffside rental. Tuesday evening, Dave calls me from work to tell me that Thaddeus, another old friend of mine from Dundee days, died on Saturday (May 22), at his home. Like Natalie, Thad appears in *Dreaming Myself, Dreaming a Town*[1] as an unexpected recollector of dreams ("two and three a night, sometimes more!"). And here, again in odd connection with Natalie's dream, I find out about his death some time after the fact and in a "secondhand manner," as Dave, who has distant in-law ties with Thad's family, had heard the news from a third party, and not, say, directly from Thad's relatives or from print or radio obituaries.

Moreover, there is a strange coincidence of place going on here. Thad's house is on the same road (and overlooks the same precipice) as the rental where Dave and I had just spent the same weekend and which seemed to connect so neatly with the scene in Natalie's dream— in which she and I had been arguing about whether or not Ann, herself a former cliffside lake dweller, had died. A dream Natalie had told me the day after Thad had died (unbeknownst to us), and in the house just down the road from where I was staying. (Perhaps I'd even been there at the time of his leave-taking, as it were.) To add to that, Thad's *house* is specifically mentioned in *Dreaming Myself*.[2]

Such a swirl of known and unknown events, juxtaposed by time and place, coincidence and dreams—it was almost too complex for words, or any form of linear thought. Clearly, there was information here for the gleaning. But why this particular information? As much as I'd liked Thad and Ann, we weren't close friends. I hadn't seen either one of them in at least ten years. What was this about? Something tugged at me, some connection I'd forgotten; something more than the serendipity of just-by-chance renting a place so close in time and space to Thad's last moments, and the element of Natalie's dream. Maybe all of this represented some sort of amorphous communication from Thad, something I was only able to discern through this evocative volley of coincidence. A far-out notion, maybe, but certainly the sort of thing that would give Thad a chuckle. Anything to confound the liberal!

So I paw through my records, not knowing what I'm looking for, exactly—and suddenly there it is, in my own notes, forgotten and yet evoked; a conversation I'd had with Natalie three months before, in early February. We'd run into one another in the Watkins Glen P&C, and it was two separate conversations, actually; one in the grocery aisles and one in the checkout lane, where we'd also happened to converge simultaneously.

Very peculiarly—I'm astonished, reading this—I'd started the first conversation that day by telling Natalie how I used to run into Ann's husband in the same supermarket (obviously they had to be living in their nearby lake home at the time), and how he was constantly bugging me about the (to me utterly boring) manuscript he'd written on bureaucratic issues, and the evasive measures I'd developed (such as hiding in the store's bathroom) to avoid him. I'd recounted this to Natalie as an amusing story, connected with a funny remark Ann had once made about writers and social workers as couples. As I stood there going on about this to Natalie, I'd had no idea (I now realized, reading this) that Ann was dead, though I did notice that Natalie stared at me in a strange way, without reply, as if I were speaking in tongues, or something. Of course, the reason for her reaction was that by then *she* knew that Ann had died, but didn't know that *I* didn't know, and *wouldn't* know until three months later, when Natalie herself would inform me of this fact in the restaurant.

We'd gone our separate grocery shopping ways, and as I headed for the checkout and saw that Natalie was going to be waiting in line ahead of me, it occurred to me (according to my notes) to ask her if she'd heard about the recent death of our friend "Al," a well-known figure in Dundee, who also appears in *Dreaming Myself*. Al had died suddenly in January, and I don't know why the impulse came to me to ask Natalie if she knew about it, other than the fact that she'd been living in Watkins Glen for several years by then and I thought she might not have heard about it or seen the obituary. And indeed, she had not—she had no idea that Al had died, and when I told her, she looked completely pole-axed (as my notes describe her expression).

"No," she finally stammered, "you're joking." Well, no, I wasn't.

And now, reading these notes, a bundle of connections fell into place, not to mention questions. Natalie hadn't quite "disputed the fact" of Al's death, but her first (understandable) reaction was complete disbelief. We'd both conveniently forgotten this supermarket scene by the time of our restaurant conversations and Natalie's dream. And why was that? Really, how much alike could all these scenes be, for crying out loud? You couldn't write this up as a piece of fiction—nobody would believe it!

To me, anyway, there was a huge cluster of coincidental material here, not all of it precognitive in the usual sense (as Natalie's dream must have drawn from a memory of our P&C meeting), but moving toward something nonetheless, almost relentlessly. Each piece fairly shimmered with allusion to the others: the act of going about food business between snippets; settings reminiscent of other occasions, both pleasant and not; death coming as a surprise and yet heralded, too; even a reference to my old book, in which many of the same people had talked to me about dreams and coincidence. And whatever the source, Natalie had dreamed about me the night before our happenstance meeting in the restaurant, a neat hit in itself. In fact, it was this "hit" that had set the whole cluster off, at least from my viewpoint, like an intuitive key appearing at just the right moment.

Moreover the core of this cluster held a definite sense of gathering-up, of acknowledgements and good-byes exchanged, rather like a small-town wake—but on other levels of association, using time and space in evocative ways to make these connections, as coincidence does so effortlessly. Not so far-fetched to think of consciousness sending a "forward to all" farewell as it departs the realm, and us interpreting the message in a kind of clairvoyant whirlpool of synchronistic imagery.

Still, something more was going on in these coincidence-encounters between Natalie and me, something that seemed important beyond an exchange of information. As many people know from their own experiences of it, death awareness (knowing that someone has died or is about to die) isn't all that unusual, and its expression ranges from vague feelings to explicitly direct intuitive information, including dream information. Usually we think of this as a one-on-one sort of communication, a natural side effect of not wanting to let go, which is why this flurry of shared interconnections intrigued me so much. It was as if the cluster itself had expanded the boundaries of the moments in which they occurred to offer a glimpse, a sensory experience, of the wider, spacious present: the iceberg that coincidence so often represents, this one with death awareness at its core.

This wasn't the first time I'd come across a synchronistic collection of spacious-present "bits" in group form. In 1979, as I relate in *Dreaming Myself*, a couple dozen people in Dundee (Thad included) came to me with dreams that when pieced together formed a very evocative foretelling of a local man's drowning. Individually, the dreams were like tiny facets of that event (an upturned boat on dark waters, a figure standing in fog by the lakeshore) but taken as a whole the sense of group precognition, everyone contributing what they could, was undeniable. Dreams that occurred after the man's death seemed to me as precognitive as the ones preceding it, though of course how could they be? Only later did I realize I'd somehow managed to capture a coincidence cluster as it emerged through the consciousness of an entire town—captured a group experience of the spacious present, in fact, as it unfolded around the hub of death awareness.

Well, death and birth are the stories that come true for all of us, so it's hardly surprising that coincidence, precognition, and our other native senses would rise up around them. Maybe the simple act of turning your attention in this direction affects you forever, changes you on a cellular level, sparks an evolutionary momentum—the mind upgrading itself, and who knows what other tendrils of association might rise to the surface of our minds to represent it.

12

An Odyssey of Letters
Coincidence Illuminating the Past

I t's early November, 1999, and I'm in the midst of working on my memoir, *Speaking of Jane Roberts*. I've decided to use excerpts from a collection of letters that Rob Butts (Jane's husband) exchanged with Jane's first husband, Walter Zeh, after her death in 1984. Rob has sent me a copy of the complete correspondence, in which the two men compare their memories. It's a masterpiece portrait not only of a unique woman but of days long vanished over the horizon of time, and I'm grateful to have access to it.

Reading these letters has been a profound experience in many ways, and not just for the glimpses of a young Jane. For one thing, it's remarkable how much alike the two men are in writing style, point of view, and life experience. Well, they're of an age, I think—Rob had turned 80 that June—so how old would Walt be today? If he's still alive, that is. Is he? I don't know. Briefly I consider calling Rob to ask this question (though I never do). The image I've created of Walt, conjured from reading his words, floats in my mind. A golden light seems to surround this made-up figure, and I realize that I feel a strong obligation toward him in regard to my book. For my purposes, on this project the Fair Use rule applies, so I don't need to secure permission—and Walt has already been mentioned in Jane's other books, so it isn't as if I'd be outing him in some way. But I don't want to surprise him, either. If nothing else, it's plain good manners to communicate with him about this.

I write Walt a letter, using the fifteen-year-old address from the correspondence, introducing myself and explaining my project. I'm not asking for permission, exactly; it's approval I want from him. In some way, I've come to like Walt very much, though we've never met. And yet I never mail the letter. I put it on a corner of my desk, where it sits for a few days, and when I look at it again I think that maybe I should figure out which excerpts I want to use, and how they're going to fit in the manuscript, before sending it to him. Before I know it, with one thing and another, almost three weeks go by and Walt's letter still sits there. Finally on November 30 I spiff it up a little and update it, and then I put it back down on my desk. And again, for some reason, I just don't get around to mailing it.

As it turned out, that indecision (Didn't Do X, which Leads to Y) had its own logic. In early December I found out that Walt had died on November 11, 1999,[1] in the same timeframe I'd been thinking of him so strongly, wondering if he were still alive. Wondering how he'd feel about excerpts from his letters appearing in my memoir. Feeling a connection with him that sprang from a time and place, not to mention a person, that our lives had each contained. And then I'd put my letter to him aside. Almost as if I'd known it was too late to reach him. By the usual methods, anyway.

Had I picked up on Walt's death, in some coincidence of thought and circumstance? Had he stopped by on his way out, responding in his gracious way to my feeling that I owed him a communication? Well, in my mind this sort of thing is not only possible, but goes on all the time—in a way, the question might be, why wouldn't this be so? Why wouldn't we be aware of everyone's death, and birth too for that matter, on some level? Of course conscious acknowledgement of such information would depend, like everything else, on intent and on something else, something involving the sheer necessity of focus, that seems embedded in the moments from which these coincidence tales always seem to spring.

All quite evocative, to say the least, and I kept thinking of Walt from time to time through the months and various editing procedures leading up to my memoir's publication in the fall of 2000. Then in April 2001, I received an email on my publisher's website from Karl Zeh, one of Walter's sons. I'd never met Karl (or any of Walt's family), so I was quite surprised by his friendly email. He'd come across a Net-search reference to *Speaking of Jane Roberts* and wanted to know if Jane had ever talked about his father, and if I'd mentioned Walt in my book (which obviously he hadn't read).

Mentioned him! Wait until you hear this, I thought, and in my reply to Karl (assuring him for one thing that Jane had indeed spoken occasionally, and well, of Walt) I told him about the letters I'd excerpted in the memoir. I also told him about the coincidence of my thoughts about Walt around the time of his death, and the letter I'd never sent. All of this was fascinating to Karl, too, so I arranged to send him a copy of his father's correspondence with Rob. According to Karl, Walt ". . . kept those years of his life very much to himself; rarely, if ever, speaking of them, or Jane." Later he wrote to me that the letters contained many details of Walt's early life that his family had never known before, and thus delivered, as you might imagine, a profoundly moving experience "beyond words," as Karl described it.

Which was something else about this whole business that I'd been ruminating about since Karl's first email to me. He'd pointed out the interesting significance of Walt's death date (November 11, Veteran's Day), as he'd served with much pride in the Army Air Corps during World War II. Reading that, it occurred to me that my own father's death date, December 13 (in 1983), was close to the date,

December 19 (in 1941), when he (along with thousands of others) had enlisted in the Marine Corps, at the heartbreakingly young age of twenty-one. Death dates as statements of loyalty, of obligations to those gone before?

Like Walt, my father never talked about that time in his life, except for one or two carefully-chosen (I now realize) humorous anecdotes. He had been among the first wave of Marines to invade Guadalcanal in August 1942, and later served as a drill sergeant and demolitions expert at the military base near Santa Barbara, California, where my parents were married in 1943. All these facts I'd gleaned from family stories and the extensive archives of family papers I dug out of my parents' attic in 1986.

What I didn't have was any sense of the person my father had been in those years, the person who had more or less vanished by the time I knew him. How I envied Walt's son, thinking how wonderful it would be to find some letters written by my father or about my father that would open up the past for me in the way that collection had for the Zeh family. Though I'd always sensed a deep appreciation of the mysterious in my father, the sort of thing I at least associate with writers, I'd never come across anything (aside from college papers) written by him or, for that matter, about him.[2]

Over the next few weeks, sparked by the exchange with Karl, these thoughts grew into a heightened yearning and I spent hours sorting through the boxes of paper ephemera (some of it more than a hundred years old), hoping to find something that would illuminate my father's life during the war years. I knew that his best friend Benny had been killed in the South Pacific, though nothing else had ever been said about it. Thus it was a poignant surprise to come across a photo of the two of them, a couple of ten year olds sitting on a home-made soapbox car in a peaceful Elmira lawn, happy pals growing up together. A few other pictures of Benny, one with a goofy-looking old dog, were stuck in the back of a scrapbook. Attached to this last was an announcement of Benny's engagement to an Elmira girl and two news clips from the local paper about his death by sniper bullet in New Guinea in March of 1944. That was all.

These told me a great deal, but except for a copy of my father's honorable discharge certificate (itself a small gem), I found nothing in words about him that I hadn't already read. For some reason I couldn't accept this. I sifted through everything a second and then a third time, urged on by an inexplicable certainty that some lost treasure would materialize. But my quest was fruitless. In a way, I knew more about Benny's wartime youth than I did about my father's.

In the midst of this, I decide one evening in early May to drive into town and see the movie, "O Brother, Where Art Thou," which has finally come to the little theater in Watkins Glen. It's a modern fable loosely based on Homer's *Odyssey*, the immortal ninth-century epic in which the hero Odysseus has many adventures while trying to get home from the Trojan wars before his wife gives up on him and marries someone else. I know the essential story, having read it in high school and college, but soon enough I realize that the movie is making many sly references to the original that are flying right over my head. Disgraceful! I'll just have to settle for ogling George Clooney until I can reeducate myself on the pertinent allegorical derivations, that's all.

So as soon as I get home I go into my library to find a copy of *The Iliad* and *The Odyssey*, thinking I'll reread it and then see the movie again. Many of my books are classics passed down to me from parents and grandparents, including textbooks from my mother's college courses in Greek and Roman history. Somewhere amongst them should be her copy of *The Odyssey*. I start scanning through the titles.

Then for some reason—I don't know why—I reach up to the top shelf and pick out a fat tome entitled *The Stories of the Greeks*, by Rex Warner.[3] I literally have not so much as touched this book, let alone opened it, in the fifteen years since I cleaned out my parents' house. In fact, this moment in 2001 is probably the first time I've ever opened the book in my life, because when I flip its pages to the index, four small brown envelopes fall out on the carpet by my feet.

They are V-mail from World War II, all addressed to my father, copied and approved by a military censor from the War and Navy Departments. I have never seen these letters before, had no idea they'd been waiting for me all these years in a book about Greek mythology. The shock and surprise I feel leave me almost unable to open the envelopes. My hands are shaking so much that I have to clench my fists and calm myself down before I dare pull the brittle sheets out and unfold them.

The letters are all dated in the fall of 1943, and three of them are from Benny. Of course I know that Benny will die within months of writing these words, because I've just spent weeks looking through every scrap of paper I could find about my parents' experience of World War II. The fourth letter is from another friend of my father's, stationed somewhere in Europe. The writing styles are straightforward, without anguish or complaint. All are writing to congratulate my father on his recent marriage, and to reminisce about home and friends and the great times they've had, and will have again, after they all come home from the war. The details are homey, even mundane. Yet as I read them something opens in the air, in my heart. For a moment my father comes alive in the time and place evoked by those letters: Twenty-three, just married, so young it makes you cry to imagine it, in the midst of a war in which he'd already endured the horrors of Guadalcanal (and could have been shipped overseas again at any time, as these letters indicate).

And throughout, all of them want only one thing, the universal, timeless thing: to come home, like Odysseus; to get back to wives and girlfriends and old familiar hangouts and good times before it all vanishes forever, though nothing would ever be the same.

The feelings I experience while reading those letters is indeed, as Karl Zeh had put it, beyond words, as much for the specific timing of this coincidence as anything else. I didn't find them six months before the email from the Zeh family, or a year later, browsing through my book collection—but right *now*, in this specific moment. Moreover, they weren't tucked away in a logical place, such as in the many folders of old letters and newspaper clippings that were, in fact, part of the family papers I'd been searching. And they could have been letters from any of my father's pals in the service, but no: three were from the lost best friend about whom I'd just been thinking, whose ghostly presence has in fact always affected me deeply, as much for my identification with the idea of best friends as the implacable drama of war and its consequences that Benny's loss represents.[4]

Furthermore, the letters had been stuck in a book that I never would have opened for this specific purpose in a million years. I can't say why I reached up for it, or what whisper of association I might have made as I did so, except that embedded in this startling coincidence is the plot of a movie based on a tale about warriors trying to make their way home and maybe salvage something of their old lives. Interesting that for both Karl Zeh and me, each set of previously unknown letters and their accompanying revelations about our respective fathers had appeared in our lives spontaneously, while searching out a book. "Stories of the Greeks," indeed!

For me, why this particular book? Who put those old letters in there, anyway? Written on its title page in my mother's hand is "To Liz [my mother's nickname], Xmas, 1968." So it was a Christmas present, but from whom? The "Liz" designation suggests it might have been from my father, but this self-inscription is very odd, as if my mother were back-dating a memory (as I was trying to do now, actually). Had she unearthed the letters herself from somewhere and stuck them in Warner's book for who knows what reason? If so, it's possible that I watched her do this and consciously forgot it until all these years later, when some part of my mind finally managed to connect a maze of dots and come up with the fleeting impulse to haul that dusty unread book off the shelf.

Even in those terms, this is a nifty feat of consciousness, scrolling through the decades to locate something, anything, written about my father's war years. But the timing of it, and the method, as if meant to derive all the meaning possible from the experience rather than just "remember" where the letters were hiding, is even more extraordinary. From my unsent letter to Walt and his death on Veteran's day in 1999 to his son's inquiry to me, searching for his father's history, to this moment of discovery in 2001 moments after I return from seeing a movie update of the iconic epic of men returning home from war, it's as if an entirely new story has been told, or written; a story emerging anew, in the spacious present, to illuminate the past. And all of it centered on a series of charged coincidental events set out before me in smooth answer to my quest.[5]

13

My Brain Goes to the Moon
Coincidence Changing the Past

Sifting through the mass of family papers in search of information about my father made something else a lot clearer: I had a job on my hands. Aside from the revelations of war letters, this experience scared me a bit. What if these irreplaceable records, generations of homey lists and postcards, school notices and bankbooks, obits and birth announcements, moldered away on my watch? They needed to be taken out of cardboard and filed in archival containers. Besides, I was about to put my house on the market and I needed to organize this accumulation into something neat, as well as more easily transportable.

Thus my self-appointed task in the winter of 2003 was to get this stuff in order. In a way, going through these papers was like writing a book. Every scrap held a story, either in itself or by inference. Stories of individuals, and of history, but most of all family stories; anecdotes I recalled and hints of tales I'd never know. And now it was up to me to preserve them.

It's a strange, urgent feeling, as anyone who's ever embarked on personal history knows. And the process does something to you that's at once obvious and yet profoundly mysterious. For years that dour, detached expression your great-grandmother wears in all those sepia

photos implied a difficult, unpleasant personality. The dark and brood-
ing oil paintings she left behind, desolate with gnarled tree branches
and solitary animals, roses fallen from their bouquets, would seem to
confirm this diagnosis. Now you find a death certificate for a previously unknown week-old baby, and another story emerges. Her life
opens up. The photos show something else. The past has changed.

Not to mention your present.

In the midst of this strange archeology, somewhere in a box of old
report cards and high school diplomas, I come across a story of my own
that I'd written twelve years before, and forgotten. Why I put it in this
specific box I'm not sure, though as I look it over I remember that I
became disgusted with it, and ashamed, so I hid it. Shame is a particularly cruel curse that writers often feel, and looking at this story now, I
recall the circumstances of its creation and demise all too clearly.

I'd just stepped out of my car near the post office in Dundee, and
who should be walking along the sidewalk but a friend I'll call Sarah, and
her four-year-old daughter Emily. Sarah and I chatted a bit—I hadn't
seen her since Emily was an infant—and that was it, nothing remarkable,
except that Emily later drew a sweet child's-eye picture of the three of us
standing together, which her mother sent to me in the mail. I intended
to write a little note back to Emily, thanking her for the drawing, but put
it off too long, and the next thing I knew weeks had gone by before I
thought of it again, and oh hell, I griped to myself, what's with me, anyway? Sometimes my brain just goes to the moon! Which sparked an idea,
which I put together in what I thought was a funny tale about my brain
taking a vacation to the moon and my cats and some crows flying up
there to bring me home. I illustrated it with silly magic marker drawings,
titled it, "A Letter to Emily," and mailed it out the next day.

But Sarah returned it to me without showing it to her daughter. As
she'd noted on a piece of paper clipped to the pages, Sarah thought the
idea of a detached brain wandering around was "too grotesque" for Emily
to read. Looking at this story now, in 2003, I remember how exquisitely

humiliated I'd felt by this remark. The note was gone, but I recall it too well, and my own self-admonishment. Who did I think I was, anyway, sending pictures of brains with feet to somebody else's child?

Secretly, though—and I begin to remember this, too—I was also plenty pissed at Sarah for shattering my exuberance. While writing the "Letter," I'd considered sending it to a few children's book publishers, too. Finding it in my mailbox that day, summarily rejected by Sarah's reply, had nixed that idea in a hurry. After that, I somehow never got around to communicating with Sarah or her daughter again. And a little seed of resentment, fueled by shame, took root.

Funny, coming across that old story now, mixed in with all my ancestor papers. It occurs to me that I must not have opened this box a year and a half ago, when I was searching for tidbits about my father's life; or else in my intense focus on that I'd overlooked this tale (and it a "letter" at that!). At least I hadn't thrown the thing away. Maybe I can still do something with it, I muse. The sense of disapproval from Emily's mother still lingers on it, though, like a bad smell, so I put it back in the box and go on with my sorting.

The next afternoon, a snowy Saturday, I decide to catch a ride with a friend to Penn Yan to pick up the laminator I'd ordered by phone from the bookstore there. The laminator has been in for more than a week, and I want it specifically to preserve the old newspaper clippings and other papers, but the weather has been lousy lately, and I hate driving anywhere in wintry conditions. It's only because of a complicated thread of changed plans and coincidental happenstance that I have the chance to ride over with this friend, so I grab it while I can. Not only will I be able to pick up the laminator, I'll have an hour or so to browse in the store besides. I haven't been in the place for at least a year, if not longer, and it always has a great selection of books and office supplies (including scrapbook materials, just what I need for this project). Definitely worth the forty-five white-knuckle minutes along icy, snow-blown highways and byways to get there.

The trip over is every bit as miserable as I'd expected, but walking in the bookstore is like opening the door to the land of Oz. I wander blissfully among the shelves for maybe half an hour, and have just worked my way around to the scissors, paste, and glue section when the front door opens, and in walks none other than Emily's mother.

To say that I nearly pass out on the floor is an understatement. Sarah and I have not seen or talked with one another since that day on the sidewalk twelve years ago that inspired my fiasco of a story, which I'd come across just yesterday after all this time. My own presence here is a result of chance and impulse, and not a little persuasion, as the bookstore was out of the driver's way somewhat, and it's only because of last-minute circumstances that he'd decided to make the trip at all. Had it not been for the weather I would have driven it myself, days ago, when the laminator first came in. And Sarah and her family still live in Dundee, so she has just navigated the same unpleasant road conditions to get here herself.

I am, therefore, stunned in triplicate. The moment I see her come in the door, a realization flashes through my head in brilliant Technicolor headlines. Of course! *This* is why you "happened" to tuck that story in amongst your ancestor papers! That facility of prescience and coincidence, combined with some other meaning, some—reason. *That's* what this is all about! With it, I have a sudden, very odd sensation that the floor is rippling under my feet, as if I were standing on a gently moving river. Yes indeed, my thoughts chirp—it's the river of time. The river of time as it changes course. A memory of my great-grandmother's face, her mouth set, eyes dim with sorrow, rises up in smooth response.

Yes. *That* river.

Sarah heads for the back register without noticing me, so I can either follow my impulse to rush over and say hello, or I can follow my equally urgent impulse to hide behind the greeting card rack until she leaves. It's a definite fork-in-the-road sensation. I think about her reaction to my "Letter to Emily" all those years ago. "Too grotesque," she'd written, and maybe that meant more than just the story. I remember my shame, and I also remember my resentment. In fact I'm suddenly furious about it all over again. How dare she call me grotesque! What nerve! I was only trying to be nice to her daughter! Umbrage starts ratcheting up, like a thumbscrew. I'm so mad I'm getting a headache.

Then I recall the little progression of this coincidence; of finding that old story, and then running into her now, the very next day, by apparent chance. Something's going on here, but what? If nothing else, I tell myself, why not see where this path might lead? The worst that can happen is she'll tell you to go pound salt. But as I thread my way through the shelves toward Sarah, my prickly thoughts begin to recede. Nah, I think, she's too polite to tell me off—that's more like something I'd do, just walk up and tell *her* to go pound salt. Which strikes me as funny, all this nattering, and for what? A twelve-year old remark, meant innocently enough? By the time I come up behind her, where she's standing at the counter going through a large textbook, I feel a wave of affection for my old friend.

"Hey, Sarah," I say, and she turns around, and her eyes light up and fill with tears! She gives me a big hug! "Oh, how are you?" she blurts. "It's been so long!"

Zeus on a cracker, I think, what is *this*? I'm shocked and surprised all over again. Of course, I can't resist telling her that just yesterday I found that story she'd disliked so much all those years ago, and I'd come all the way over here today on impulse and chance, and then we run into one another, and isn't that funny, and . . .

"What story is that?" she asks.

Great, not only was the damn thing grotesque, it was forgettable, and which is worse? "Oh, it was about my cats and some crows and my brain all going to the moon," I shrug. "I drew some pictures for it and mailed it to Emily, but you didn't think it was right for her, so you sent it back to me."

She stares at me blankly. "I don't remember that at all," she says. "I'd *love* to see it, though! Why don't we have coffee sometime and catch up, and you can show it to me? I'd really like to see *anything* you've written!"

"Uh—sure," I say, a bit dumbfounded. What just happened? Not only has my friend forgotten her previous reaction to my story—not only has she forgotten the entire incident—I'm realizing with some discomfort that the resentment I'd so carefully harbored has vanished like a soap bubble, and not only because of her apparent change of heart. Really, I can't even recall why I was so irked with her in the first place. After all, I'd be the last person to second-guess a mommy's judgment, wouldn't I? Maybe I'd misremembered. Or . . . maybe the whole thing didn't happen at all. Had I—blatantly made it up? Or had I—*unmade* it up? Or what?

Weirdly, on the heels of this thought, I again feel that sensation of the floor rippling gently. Either the past is opening up or I'm having a fainting spell. But no, I'm fine, standing here returning Sarah's beaming smile. Somehow or other, a new story (about a story) is moving out in all directions, from this moment in my present into my past, but also from the past into this moment, and into the future as I think of it. Or something like that, almost inexpressible—the feeling of the spacious present, coming alive. It's a heady sensation, triggered by coincidence and a willingness on my part to take a small social risk inspired by it. And who knows, maybe Sarah associates me with some social risk, too; for one thing she teaches in a Christian school whose members would view me (at least theoretically) with disapproval, I suppose.

Still, she says she likes my writing, and I'm always willing to bank on that, and the moment is whirling around and around as we stand there and I'm thinking how I'll have to write this up the minute I get home when Sarah asks me if I'm working on something new these days and I decide to half-lie by saying, "More or less."

She gives me a look, and says, "Are you happy?" And without thinking I say, "No." What? What was *that*! Quickly, I add, "It's just a stagnant time in my writing life while I'm waiting for things to resolve with putting my house on the market," but even to my ears, this sounds phony. Sarah says nothing, continues to stare at me. "I'll get back to it," I say, lame as a duck. "Really, I will. I promise!"

Sarah laughs, says she'll make a deal with me: I should come over to her house someday soon and bring the "Letter to Emily" and whatever else of my stuff I'd like her to read. I don't know if I'll actually do this, but what's important here is that personal history has been rewritten before my eyes; affirmation has been exchanged. As if to reinforce this, I notice that the textbook Sarah is hanging onto is for some kind of online Master's program in library science. Interesting that a couple days ago I'd read a piece from a back issue of *The New Yorker* by a woman who was in the process of getting a Master's in library science, something that's always interested me, too.

Sarah and I say our goodbyes at this point—my friend's truck has just pulled up at the curb outside—and I leave the store in a dazed reverie about the inner workings of this particular outer event. Nothing world-shattering, and nothing that doesn't happen every day, memories changing in various ways large and small. Did our encounter change the past or change my memories of the past? Is there a difference?

On one hand it seems clearly nuts to suppose that the actual, carved-in-stone past can be altered, and modern whack efforts such as Holocaust denial make me reluctant to speculate to the contrary. On the other hand, the fact is we have no clear idea of what the "past" is, of how we retain it and what it actually includes from the individual's perspective, which is my interest here. Sarah's memory was no less vivid than mine and yet each was as different from one another's as the proverbial night and day. I'd lost her written note, so I had no "proof" of her role in my recollection. Maybe I'd even imagined the note in the first place. What if we could "misremember" the horrors of the past in the same way? What benefits would we reap?

But for now we're a species that must in this time and place remember our history or condemn ourselves to repeat it. Still, catching a hint of other possibilities through the prism of coincidence, and having the chance to renew a friendship thereby—and experiencing a sense of the spacious present's vibrant capacities—now that's a story to remember. I might even start sending "A Letter to Emily" around to a few publishers while I'm at it. Even if it is grotesque!

14

The San Francisco Quake of '89
When Coincidence and Mass Events Collide

The following coincidence cluster involves the fiercest precognitive intuitions in the world—those of a mother looking out for her son, who in the fall of 1989 at the too-tender age of nineteen decided to cram all of his stuff, including his motorcycle, into a U-Haul and take off for the wilds of San Francisco and a certain jazz singer named Cindy.

You are never, believe me, ready for them to leave. Since graduating from high school, Sean had been living at home and clerking in a Sam Goody's record store in Elmira, and while this was hardly the pinnacle of my fondest hopes for him, I'd somehow never quite believed that he'd take off on his own. What? All the way across the country by himself? Out into the world? All the way to California? And with that damned motorcycle of his?

I hated that motorcycle. It was a bright red Yamaha Radian 600, the kind any mother would like to shove into a nearby muck-pond, and I had seriously considered doing just that. Though he wasn't driving it to California, Sean couldn't wait to get out there with it (out there in California traffic!) and zoom all over the place on it.

He'd already dumped the thing a couple of times. In fact, the last time this had happened, just days before he left for San Francisco, a little girl dashed out in front of him on a side street in Dundee; and though Sean managed to slam on the cycle's brakes in time, he'd sailed up and over the handlebars, road-rashed his knees and forehead, ripped up his leather jacket, and crunched the Yamaha's gas tank to the tune of about two hundred dollars (not nearly enough damage, in my opinion). This happened on Sunday, September 24, 1989.

The next morning, I recorded this dream: "There's a *thing* under the ground. Some kind of *thing*. As it moves, it causes the ground to heave up. It's all over the place. Suddenly, a mass of tentacles pokes through the ground and waves all around, reaching, reaching. Eeeek!"

Years later, looking this over, I would think—right there was the first link between Sean's motorcycle and the earthquake, though not exactly in a precognitive way. Here, the incident (motorcycle accident) happened first, the dream (of a "thing" moving the ground) second. Not a coincidence in the usual sense, either. But, a link. An intuitive association. With something. But what?

Sean left for California on Monday, October 2. Saying good-bye was fairly devastating, as you might imagine. For the next two nights, I dreamed that I *was* Sean, driving across the country, through plains and mountains, safe in the U-Haul. "The feeling is protective," my dream record says, "as though I'm 'becoming' Sean to get him out there safe and sound."

Three days later, on Thursday, October 5, part of the dream I recorded for that night involved this little scene: My late father appeared before me wearing Sean's purple Sam Goody's shirt from his record store job, the shirt that Sean had actually been wearing when I took a photo of him standing in front of the Yamaha the day before he left for California. Several other people were in this dream, all wearing clothes that "actually" belonged to others—a big dream-emphasis on mixed-up clothing. And then, in the dream, I realized this: Sean, out in

California, was in the midst of a big earthquake, and I had to go find him and get him out of there. This message was clear and explicit.

I didn't take this as a precognitive warning. I was far more intrigued by the mixed-clothing bit, especially the appearance of my father wearing Sean's shirt. After all, it's only natural to worry about earthquakes, waking *or* dreaming, when your baby has just left for San Andreas Fault country. So I dismissed that portion of the dream as ordinary, a product of my explainable motherly fears. What I took from the dream instead was the idea of my father's incredibly lucky nature reaching out to Sean on that vile motorcycle. My father had been a pilot in his younger years and had engaged in some truly mind-boggling feats in his single-engine Piper (landing in wheat fields and on highways, etc.) without mishap; at nineteen, Sean was a pilot of both gliders and power planes, and seemed to possess the same kind of flying wits and fortune. But it wasn't Sean's airplane-piloting adventures that scared me. No, my anxieties were focused exclusively on the motorcycle.

So I found this mixed-up clothing dream to be quite reassuring about it all. That afternoon, Sean called me from a friend's house in Oakland. He'd made it just fine, in good time. So that's taken care of, I told myself. Aren't dreams neat?

Yeah.

As I've mentioned, one notion that occurred to me while I was writing *Dreaming Myself, Dreaming a Town* was that precognition is not so much a literal re-creation of paranormally perceived future events as it is a tightly interwoven collection of information, weaving and crisscrossing among dreams, coincidences, random thoughts and impulses, all of which come together to more or less suggest the event in question. It also seemed to me that the actual precognition had more to do with significance than literal re-creation, though that's involved too. Emotional preparation (as several people remark in the book) seems to be the central purpose of such attributes, in that each tidbit or cluster carries its own clue about the nature of the (perhaps only probable) upcoming events, sometimes even displaying the *why* of the event, in a language all its own.

All observable only if you keep track of this sort of thing in the first place, a truly endless endeavor. Every time I look through my dream journals, I see more connections and coincidences than I did the time before. It's as though the dreams and interconnecting events are still ongoing back there, continuing to grow and interweave with my present moments.

So again, how much do we know, and when (and how) do we know it? What happens, exactly, at the point of "knowing?" How precognitive is every single dream; how far does any given coincidence reach? Does every dream, and every moment in linear time, contain information about everything that will happen, or might happen? Do these events continue to expand back there in the past; do they keep filling up with information as our present moments update the significance of every dream, every coincidence we ever experience?

You could speculate endlessly. Which is the approximate amount of time you'd need to keep records of it all. After a while, it's overwhelming—your brain begins to hurt, not to mention your typing fingers. Which might be why I didn't pay more attention as the dreams and quake bits began to accrue. Or, very possibly—I just didn't want to know anything about this on a conscious level. Would you?

Tuesday, October 10: I dream that my uncle Bob (who died in 1988) calls me up to give me "some kind of warning." But upon waking I can't recall what sort of warning he had to give.

Later that afternoon, my aunt Marie—sister of my uncle Bob and my mother—calls me up to chat, which is interesting enough, since I haven't talked with her in quite a while, and here she is calling me the day after I dream about her brother. She tells me that she and her husband are traveling to Hawaii in a couple of weeks, and they'll be staying overnight in San Francisco on October 24, and could they have Sean's phone number? Maybe they'll stop and see him, she says.

Then, according to my notes, Aunt Marie tells me she's been reading *Dreaming Myself, Dreaming a Town*. I'm surprised by this, and a little nervous about her reaction. But she says, "You and I think more alike than either of us ever knew," and I'm immediately reassured. She goes on to specifically mention a dream of Sean's that I'd included in the book[1]—a dream about an earthquake, when he was thirteen years old. Waking from that dream, on May 25, 1983, Sean had told me that he "knew" there would be a major quake somewhere in the world within a week. The next day, a quake of 7.7 occurred in Japan. What a coincidence! And a neat piece of precognition, I'd thought at the time.

"So I guess he's got his own radar about those things, like the animals," my aunt says to me, and I admit to her that in the days since Sean left, I've spent some time moping over a map of the San Francisco area, imagining that I would move out there someday myself. I mention that I'd happened to spy a little town named Hollister, just south of the Bay area, and funny how the name is the same as the street in Dundee where I'd lived while writing the dream book. I give her Sean's San Francisco phone number and we hang up.

I make notes in my dream journal.

I forget about it.

Four days later, Saturday morning, October 14, I recorded this dream from the night before: "I rescue Sean in a bright red airplane made out of Legos . . . it looks like that Lego space ship Sean made and glued together long ago. Wherever this place is, it's dark and frightening. All the lights are off, and it's far away . . . It seems to be a war zone, or a place of great danger. I find him in a tall building and tell him to come on, and I show him our bright red Lego plane which will get us out of there . . .

"We fly off in the Lego airplane, safe from all the chaos below."

Looking over this dream—well, it sort of broke my heart a little, actually. Something about lost time and old toys . . . I didn't want to think about it too much.

About noon this same day, I get a phone call from my father's sister, Aunt Bob—a nickname she was known by all her life. We haven't talked in several weeks. I mention how funny it is that four days ago I'd had a dream about talking to my dead *uncle* Bob (from the other side of the family). Aunt Bob then says, "That *is* funny, because I called to tell you a dream that *I* had." In her dream, she and I were combined into one person, and we were "safe inside a house" (her words) with Sean and my (deceased) mother. I think this is interesting, but not very significant, except for the fact that this particular aunt is telling me a dream in the first place, not a usual topic of our (infrequent) conversations.

Later that day, I drove into Dundee to have lunch with a fan who'd written to me in August asking if we could meet. Norma was driving cross-country, to New York City, from her home in Sherman Oaks, California, to board a cruise ship bound for Bermuda. Earlier in 1989 she'd had a malignant growth removed from her shinbone, and she'd decided to "take a break" (as she put it) by treating herself to a Caribbean vacation. We had a nice conversation over coffee, and I actually invited her to come back to my house for dinner—something so unusual for me that I shocked myself. Maybe it was just the small connection with California, I thought—anyone close to where Sean is . . .

That evening, as Norma and I were eating an omelet and toast dinner, a huge thunderstorm roared in from the northwest, turning the sky black and green ("like a bruise," I remarked), with awesome bolts of lightning and house-rattling thunder. I told Norma that the storm would probably spawn a tornado somewhere in the area (which, as we learned later, it did, on the east side of Seneca Lake, killing one person and wrecking several vineyards).[2] Norma seemed a little horrified at the intensity of the storm. We talked at length about possible metaphysical meanings of natural disasters, and their appearance in one's life, and why someone might want to experience such a thing. "Sean and I were in the Flood of '72, in Elmira," I told her, "and that was enough for me!" She agreed. "It's enough for me just to live in earthquake country. I sure don't want to go through one," she said. Eventually, the storm let up, and Norma went on her way at about ten o'clock.

Three days later, on the morning of Tuesday, October 17, I almost didn't write my dreams down. They seemed too insignificant to bother, except for the feeling of intensity about them. They consisted of three odd little "pods" that were about nothing more than a couple of phone calls. But I've discovered that the idea of importance can be deceptive, so I typed them up anyway:

1. Terry D. calls from Paris [where he in fact lives], and I answer the phone. He tells me that he is going to be at my house "the very next day." He repeats this several times.
2. Bruce K. [local contractor and carpenter who lives in Dundee] shows up and puts the new [planned for next summer] roof on my house. He does a really fine job, but I think . . . why now? How am I going to pay for this? Why didn't he talk to me before this? [I hadn't actually talked to Bruce in months.]
3. Bob D. [brother of Terry from dream number 1] shows up from his home in Oakland [where Sean stayed for a while after arriving in California].

Well, on the surface, these dreams were just plain blah, "about" nothing at all . . . except for the feeling I had about them, which seemed ridiculous, when I examined it. I'd had huge, complex dreams with less feeling attached to them than these little doobies, I mused. Dream-recording held its own mysteries, as I'd discovered long before this. And sometimes a dream object (or phone call) is just what it is, no more.

Still, it is very uncharacteristic of me to even consider not writing these down. And so was what I did later that evening: Instead of watching television of any kind, I rented not one but two movies (I can't think of another occasion on which I rented and watched two full-length movies in a row) and invited a friend over for the evening. I didn't see any broadcast television at all that day, in other words. I shut off any official information from the outside world. (I didn't listen to the radio, either; and the daily newspaper I subscribe to is a morning edition.)

By 11 P.M., my friend and I had watched our movies and were sitting companionably by the woodstove, reading. For some reason, though I'd read it before, I was scanning through Stephen King's book, *The Stand*—which is, you will notice, a disaster novel—and, according to the notes I made later, I was specifically reading the part in the story that is set in New York, where two characters are trying to get out of the corpse-littered city, when the phone rang. This was way past the time when anyone calls me, and should have, you would think, propelled me out of my chair. Instead, I asked my friend to answer it. Oddly, instead of picking up the cordless near our chairs, he went upstairs to the kitchen phone, way out of my earshot. All I could hear was the murmur of one-sided conversation, all in normal tones.

Then he came back downstairs and handed me these scribbled notes: "7. on Richter. 5 P.M. Joe Gallagher's brother, friend of Sean's. Sean's okay." And an Albany-area phone number.

I said, "Huh? Who's Joe Gallagher?"

And then, screaming, I leaped from my chair. Finally! After all this time! After all this information had been filtering down into my consciousness for weeks and weeks! Finally, it hit me: THERE HAD BEEN A MAJOR EARTHQUAKE IN SAN FRANCISCO! AND SEAN WAS OUT THERE IN THE MIDDLE OF IT!

Momentarily, I was quite hysterical. I was so disoriented by the scribbled notes—by who and what had happened—that it took me several minutes to get my head into the gist of the situation: Sean was okay. Sean was okay. *Sean was okay.*

Miraculously (so Sean told me later), this Joe Gallagher, a neighbor of Sean's, had managed after the quake to get through to his brother in Albany even though phone service was shut down almost everywhere in the Bay area. Sean had just happened to be in this fellow's apartment and thus had gotten the message out to me that he was okay.

I don't know what I would have done without that last-minute message (forced the Lego plane to fly out there, maybe), but by coincidence and something else, some crafty juxtaposition of knowledge and wisdom, I'd done the absolutely correct thing: I'd kept knowledge of the earthquake, which had occurred at 8 P.M. my time (and was of course the subject of TV news bulletins almost from the moment it happened), out of my official consciousness until *after* I knew that Sean was okay.

As far as my unofficial consciousness was concerned—well, in those realms, the "news" had been broadcasting at what you might call full blast for weeks. Letting me know. Getting myself ready. Reporting all kinds of associated information, even in my last-minute choice of reading materials, in which two characters manage to get away from a disaster scene unscathed.

Furthermore it occurred to me that this complete stranger Joe Gallagher, who'd delivered Sean's message, had the same last name as Bill Gallagher, a long-time friend who is a power and glider pilot and was for many years the curator of Elmira's National Soaring Museum, which is attached to the airfield where Sean had earned his glider pilot license. Not only that, but a few days before this, I'd been reading the November/December issue of *Hippocrates* magazine and I'd noticed a letter to the editor written by . . . I grabbed the magazine and turned to the letters page. My memory was correct: the letter I'd specifically noticed, and remembered for some reason—the letter that had evoked a funny kind of feeling about it—had been written by a *Joe Gallagher* from Harbor City, California! I'd taken note of the letter partly because of this last-name coincidence, but at the time I'd read it, I could tell there was more, though I couldn't figure what. (The letter was crabbing about weight-charts, and ended with a gripe about "dying before one's time," weirdly.) Was it the same person, or not? I never knew.[3]

My head was swirling. I felt dizzy and a little sick to my stomach. All the connections, all the hints in coincidence and dreams involving this truly incredible disaster began to click together in my head. Specific warnings in my dreams about this earthquake, and Sean's being in the middle of it—including the scenario of me rescuing him with his toy Lego plane (which in my dream had glided out there), and now the odd Gallagher-glider-pilot-connection-message "rescue" of my peace of mind, no small thing.

Coincidence and precognition, all leading to this: Sean was not hurt. Sean was just fine. In a way, it even seemed that Sean was playing ("toying?") with the experience of a natural disaster, and not for the first time, either. Aside from our experience in the Elmira flood of 1972[4] when he was two years old, there was the incident that previous summer, when he'd been driving along a nearby highway in the midst of a thunderstorm, and a sudden blast of powerful wind forced him off the road and shot the car roof full of hailstone holes. He was unhurt, though uncharacteristically subdued by the experience. The winds were later identified by the National Weather Service as a tornado.

Funny, that a tornado had touched down across the lake from my house the Saturday before the earthquake, and that Norma and I had talked at length about natural disasters, and why people choose to be in the midst of them.

I turned the TV to the continuous network newscasts on the quake, and more details began to connect. Seismologists were already saying that the epicenter appeared to have been near *Hollister*, California, south of the Bay area. Even my random map-moping seemed to have made a precognitive contribution.

I tried to call Sean that night, without success. I'd just have to wait until he could get through to me. But in the meantime, I knew he was all right.

The next morning, Wednesday, October 18 (the "next day," as in my dream of Tuesday the 17th), the following occurred, in this order:

1. Terry D. called from Paris, France, to ask me if I'd heard anything from his brother, Bob, in Oakland.

2. As I was watching the CBS news coverage on the scene in San Francisco, who should call me to ask if I'd heard from Sean but Bruce K.! Seems he had cousins in the Bay area and he hadn't heard from them (though it turned out they were all right, too). Then out of the blue, Bruce brought up the subject of the new roof he was scheduled to put on my house the next summer. And the thing is, my first thought when he called was that he'd want to put the roof on right then, before I was able to pay for it! I hadn't realized (or I'd forgotten) that Bruce was aware that Sean now lived in San Francisco. (I was quite touched by Bruce's concern, actually.)

So the first two pieces of my Tuesday dream had "come true." A few days later Terry's brother Bob called to tell me he was okay, specifically in case Terry called me. So in a way, dream number 3 "came true": Bob "showed up" by phone. And, is it too silly to point out his name-coincidence with my aunt and uncle Bob, both of whom were involved in strangely off-to-the-side, though definite, dream-waking earthquake connections? And the element here, of brothers or brother-like names—the Gallagher guys, and now Terry and Bob, all calling me with messages on behalf of others?

Sean finally got through to me at about two in the morning, October 19. Among other tales he had to tell about his experiences was this: At the moment the quake struck, he'd been sitting in a downtown San Francisco Laundromat, washing a mix of his own and his girlfriend's clothes. In fact, at first he thought it was off-balance washing machines shaking the floor. Which reminded me of my October 5 dream in which an earthquake "warning" was clear and explicit, but from which I'd instead focused on the symbol of *mixed clothes*. (The Laundromat, as you might expect, was in a big building, and the post-quake streets certainly did resemble a war zone, according to Sean's description of the chaos, as in my Lego airplane dream.)

As time went on, the coincidental elements surrounding all of this continued to grow. The day after the quake, Wednesday, October 18, I had an unexpected visit from Rhonda and Hal, a couple from Pennsylvania whom I hadn't seen in years. Most of the afternoon was devoted to Rhonda's lengthy description of how she'd broken her ankle two summers before, and the effect this had on her life, including the "breaking away" (her words) from her somewhat tyrannical mother. I thought of Norma and her leg condition, and her decision to "take a break" after the ordeal of her operation, and how these visitors were sandwiched around the event of the earthquake, a breaking away if there ever was one, and was *that* what Sean was up to out there, so far away from home?

And what was I doing, then?

If your life were a dream, what would it mean?

So I thought it was all over with. Sean and Cindy's San Francisco apartment hadn't been damaged, and everyone I knew in the Bay area was all right. I spent a couple of days musing about the astonishing clusters of precognitive information that had risen up out of dream and coincidence, bouncing back and forth through space and, it seemed clear, through time, attaching themselves to me like invisible burdocks for weeks before the event. And how I'd chosen not to pay conscious attention to any of it. As I'd noted before, in my dreams as well as in those of others, it was all in smooth reaction to my own best interests. Had I actually, consciously known that Sean was, or was going to be, in the middle of a 7.0 earthquake before I'd heard from him, I would have gone certifiably haywire. What I had been given—what I'd paid attention to—was the reassurance that he was okay. Which is all I gave a hoot about, of course.

But I wasn't through with me yet.

Saturday, October 28: I dream that Sean has been magically transported back to my living room sofa, where I find him curled up, sleeping, posed as I'd last seen him sleep in the days after he'd had all his wisdom teeth out just before he'd left for California. Except that in my dream, he's wearing his leather motorcycle jacket. Then dream-Sean wakes up and starts stomping around, acting pissy and petulant about something, and very unpleasantly so, quite unlike his usual easygoing self.

Here again, I almost didn't bother to write the dream down— unlike *my* usual self. I was tired of feeling bad about Sean's living so far from home, for one thing. I just didn't want to think about it any more. I spent the day writing, and later, finished with reading *The Stand*, I impulsively picked up an old copy of King's *Pet Sematary* and started to reread it. A story, you will note, that centers on a little boy who runs out into the road and is hit by a truck.

I read the book through in one sitting, into the wee hours. The next morning, Sunday, October 29, I recorded this dream: "Another earthquake. It's a huge one. I see an entire piece of California, with San Francisco's Golden Gate Bridge shining brilliantly in the center, break off and migrate southward toward Mexico. I drive out in Sean's old Hyundai [which he'd left behind] to find him and rescue him. I end up driving through Mexico to find this land mass, now stuck off-shore from the Mexican west coast."

Well, this time I watched the news, but there were no huge Golden Gate–busting quakes amid the relentless aftershocks, which were scary enough. I figured that I was just subliminally worried about that. Not to worry.

Right.

About nine o'clock that night, Sean called me from his apartment. He sounded awful, and this was the reason: On Saturday afternoon (October 28), he'd crashed his motorcycle on the Marin County side of the Golden Gate Bridge while trying to drive from Oakland to San Francisco in the midst of bumper-to-bumper traffic!

Though he quickly reassured me that he'd only suffered some cracked ribs and bruises, I was, of course, horrified. Sean said he'd been maneuvering in this traffic mess at about five o'clock (California time), when the Yamaha's engine began to heat up. "I must have panicked and opened the throttle—I'm not sure," he told me. "I guess I was pretty pissed off and impatient with all the traffic." Fortunately, he was wearing his helmet, because suddenly the cycle surged forward, out of control, and he managed to swerve it back and forth between the line of vehicles for only a few seconds before he half-fell, half-jumped, into the trunk of the nearest car, bounced off, flew through the air, and landed on his head in the road.

"I couldn't move or get my breath," he told me. "A couple of people pushed me off the highway and sort of propped me up, and left. Everybody else drove right past me, staring. I don't know who shoved my motorcycle out of the way or how long I sat there." Eventually, an ambulance arrived on the scene and took him to the hospital, where after a wait of several hours, he was X-rayed, taped up, and sent home. He was also ticketed for lack of a California license and insurance, and the police impounded the badly damaged motorcycle. The clothes he'd been carrying in the saddlebags were gone too, but oh well, he said.

"I don't plan to get it back," he said. "To hell with it."

Which was, needless to say, music to my ears. It seemed to me that he'd been incredibly lucky. He wasn't seriously injured (though just enough to give up motorcycling, hurray) and he hadn't been run over in the highway. ("Thanks, Pa," I thought, recalling the Sam Goody–shirt dream.)

However, there were more very evocative coincidences going on here. For one, Sean's accident had occurred at five o'clock, the same time as the October 17 earthquake. My October 29 dream had been about another earthquake, and me driving this time—not flying—out to rescue Sean. And my October 28 dream had looked at Sean sleeping on the couch in his motorcycle jacket, in a pose reminiscent of the last time I'd mothered him through painful times; in that dream, he'd been short-tempered and impatient, the state of mind that by his own admission had contributed to his accident.

Clearly, my protective concern had cut to the meat of the matter, which was Sean's well-being whatever he was doing, or in what mood— but especially to the meat of that motorcycle. It, and the larger event of the earthquake, had become metaphorically and precognitively mixed in my dreams and in waking coincidental mini-plays that seemed to draw on everything of related significance in my daily life, including chance reading material, random thoughts, and unexpected visitor conversations.

Like a thread of inner and outer events, wrapped around one central topic: the safety of my child. Like voices from future events, broadcast in coincidence and dreams.

So there we have it: Does the conscious mind weave in and out of all possible states, waking and dreaming, present and future and past, probing the possible and the probable, assessing its own needs and purposes along the way, perfectly adapted and perfectly adaptable? Are there no limits to the amount of information available to us? Does our everyday experience naturally, and for the most part invisibly, ride on a vast network of coincidence and precognition that can be observed and recorded?

Is the "unknown" frontier more knowable, and knowing, than we currently imagine?

And by the way, on the day I initially wrote up this entire sequence from my notes—on December 28, 1994—a 7.5 earthquake hit Japan.

Coincidentally!

15

Some Final Thoughts
And a How-To of Sorts

This above all: to playfulness be true.

Coincidence is fun, and once you turn your attention to the idea of it as meaning something, your conscious interests will begin to yield an intuitive storyboard, a "natural knowing" if you will, that contains more than the everyday recognition of something that's similar to something else. Coincidence, dreams, random thoughts, precognitive hits, more coincidence, all bouncing around, collecting information in ongoing episodes, the mind boggling the mind. Catching your notice, as it were. Waving hello from the other side of the room.

Sets of coincidental associations will cluster together for a relatively short time span, then move on to a different cluster—or an update of a previous one. Why it works this way is as interesting as the ongoing coincidences themselves (maybe ordinary conscious awareness can only take so much at a time). You think of something for no apparent reason, or dream of it, and then suddenly, bam, there it is, reflected back, often in dramatic fashion. Exterior cues such as seasonal changes, routines of school and office, the loop of habit and tradition, even if consciously forgotten, feed into random thought, for one thing; and then there is the sharpshooter fallacy at work. You think a billion thoughts in a day and draw a bull's-eye around the ones that become remarkable in hindsight. Behind it is the perception pump, pumping away. You think you're going to see something, you see it. Then you start looking for it some more. Voilà! There it is!

But this doesn't account for all of it, nor does it address the impact of significance, let alone the precognitive elements, that coincidence delivers to the individual's experience. Sharpshooting and perception pumping are legitimate criticisms, especially of conspiracy theories, and being aware of these cautions helps keep one's head above the murky waters of hogwash, but there's no reason to toss the baby out with the slop, either. You can set up your own coincidence-radar and see what happens. Why not?

First and foremost, you're going to have to write this stuff down. I know, I know, you're already keeping track of what you eat, how far you walk, how much you weigh, and using "journal" as a verb left and right. Well, throw all those records in the trash and do this for a while. Coincidental events, like dreams, are almost impossible to reconstruct from memory unless you've taken detailed notes, and even then it's often a challenge to recapture the particulars, or keep up with the inter-connecting layers that spiral out at the speed of light. But even with minimum effort, you'll soon realize what a unique record this is. It's a diary of the workings of consciousness, of the contents of your own con-sciousness, as it creates the storyboard of your daily experience. You'll be enthralled. You'll discover a new source of practical information. You'll forget all those other journals and let this one take over your life. You'll write to me about it!

In fact, you don't even need a how-to in the "how to enhance your life" respect, because your consciousness is already doing that for you as best it can, as consciousness has always done, working around our beliefs to the contrary and whatever sorry state our current events and cultural input happen to be in at any given time. Connecting with a sense of wonder can only augment this natural process, maybe even benefit the world, as any kid understands implicitly. So here are some field-note techniques and fun sort of games to help wake that connection up.

1. Start a prediction list, as described in chapter 2. Take a couple minutes in the morning to clear your mind (right after you've written down your previous night's dream, of course) and scribble a list of five or six words or phrases off the top of your head, whatever comes to you. Check back with this list later that day, and periodically thereafter—making more lists as you go. See what connects with what. Watch how the connections start creating connections. Notice the rise of precognitive bits and pieces as they appear.

Be sensible about what you call a connection, and be mindful of that word-of-the-week suggestion process, but this is your notebook, and after a while you'll be familiar with the intuitive signals that recognize what's important, even if it's just a tidbit (as with my tiny telephone dreams the night before the San Francisco quake). But if you start reading coincidence into every last little thing that happens, stretching significance not to mention credulity by the neck until dead, then you've lost something else we're supposed to be paying attention to, and that is the enjoyment of our days as they pass across the earth in all their exquisite simplicity. Too many cigars, to paraphrase old Freud, can turn into a smokescreen. Keep a balance.

2. One way to keep lists that integrate more easily with modern life is to write them up as email, either to yourself or a trusted comrade. Since email automatically records the date and time, you'll have inarguable confirmation of sequence, very handy if you ever decide to do something as crazy as try to write a book about this sort of thing. You could do them as a blog, I suppose, but yikes, people, this stuff can be explicitly personal, not only about yourself but others, and if decorum doesn't give you

caution there's the question of libel to consider. In general, my advice is to keep it to yourself, at least in raw form.

3. Toss some "little thoughts" out there and see how they bounce back. Use focused imagery to address a problem, playfully, without desperation, and don't even try to prefigure a solution. Or, as in my money-in-the-mailbox visualization, make up a story in a what-the-hell offhand way about how a solution will come to you. Imagine details, even dialogue. Someone in a suit hands you a check for one of your paintings. The two of you discuss where it's going to hang. You see it there, on the wall, luminous in a shaft of sunlight. You decide it looks pretty cool.

Then think about something else. Remind yourself of this made-up scene once in a while, but otherwise forget the whole thing. Or, just tell yourself that a solution to some problem will present itself in, say, the next few hours, and see what happens. Maybe Ralph will show up and take your comic books to town for you!

As to desperation: it doesn't work. In fact, it often backfires, since anxiety tends to focus on the problem. In that, be aware that sometimes it isn't the money or the love-life you really want, it's the magic: the coincidental wow, the feedback of precognitive hits—the affirmation from your own psyche that you exist in other realms, other levels of awareness and activity as much as you do in this one.

4. As to "little thoughts tossed out," try using random thoughts to help with something that's bugging you. Tell yourself that the next thought you have, whatever it is, will be the answer. Random thoughts can open elements in your life that you've been hiding from yourself, and set off some neat coincidental feedback, too.

Example: Some years ago, while I was in the midst of a stormy relationship (so what else is new), I woke up one morning with a crick in my neck so severe I couldn't move my head, and even my shoulders seemed frozen solid. Aspirin and heating pads did nothing for it. Only after suffering this for a couple of days did it occur to me to try this random-thought experiment, so I said to myself, "I will accept my next thought as the reason I have this neck-crick."

Immediately, and forcefully, almost vocally, that next thought was, "Because [boyfriend] is turning away from you."

I had no conscious idea that this was the case. No, that isn't true. The fact is (as I finally admitted to myself in random thought's wake) I'd refused to acknowledge what I'd known, underneath my happy assurances to the contrary, that this was exactly the case. More than that—suddenly my inner knowledge burst free—I'd known it was going to be the case from the beginning. And now it was time to accept what I knew. Within half an hour, the "pain in my neck" went away. (The other pain took somewhat longer to get rid of, but that's another story.)

Well, all the aspirin probably helped, but the point is, random thoughts act like couriers between the various compartments of the conscious mind, and as such, they play an intriguing and not infrequently amusing role in coincidence, precognition, clairvoyance, and other dreamlike aspects of waking life—not to mention providing some straightforward personal growth on occasion.

5. Keep your inner eye open for coincidence, because sometimes⸮ it flicks by before you can glimpse more than the flash of a wing, or configuration of flight. Not to impose your expectations or read into something that isn't there, but sometimes connections don't register right away, and then you've lost some of the details. Pay attention when a particular coincidence subject keeps popping up. It means something; your consciousness is broadcasting on your behalf, and you're supposed to make use of the information. This is why you need written records.

And trust me on this: they never stop interconnecting with your present moments. Weeks or years after the fact, coincidence clusters can spring to life, renewing themselves in dazzling displays, like waking recurrent dreams. Why this happens when it does is up to you to ask.

Am I just drawing the bull's-eye? Is this a mere happenstance of perception, nothing more? Or is it indicative of something else going on here, some recurring belief-situation or mechanism of reality that's important as well as astonishing?

6. Above all, be honest and accurate. Keep in mind that as with any field notes, of bird or wildflower or loops of connective events, your beliefs not only color what you see, they're part of the environment that you measure. All you can do is write it all down, maintain your common sense, and enjoy yourself. Eat a good breakfast. Wear a hat.

And leave the motorcycle behind in the garage.

Endnotes

Chapter 1: Yikes! What Was That?

1. Kim Stanley Robinson, *The Years of Rice and Salt* (New York: Bantam, 2002).

2. Evelyn died at home, on January 29, 2004, of a pulmonary embolism.

3. Sam Harris, *The End of Faith: Religion, Terror, and the Future of Reason* (New York: W. W. Norton, 2004).

Chapter 2: Conjuring the Eleemosynary

1. Which I'm selecting for the interesting hits; there are plenty in my records that have none, or I didn't bother to make note of any that did occur. See other examples in chapter 3 of my book *Conversations with Seth* (Needham, MA: Moment Point Press, 2005).

2. *Dreaming Myself, Dreaming a Town* (New York: Kendall Enterprises, 1988).

3. The urban-legends website www.snopes.com dissects these alleged connections, as well as thousands of other modern stories of conspiracy and mayhem. I also recommend the wonderful books by Jan Harold Brunvand, who was what you might call the founding father of urban-legend collection, starting with that story about "the vanishing hitch-hiker" that I absolutely know is true because it happened to my best friend's cousin's brother while driving on the river road between Elmira and Waverly back in 1956.

4. I did write a piece on precognitive dreams of that event for my author's bulletin board on the Moment Point Press website,

www.momentpoint.com, titled, "September 11, 2001, Foretold." (Which, by the way, is being used by Joseph Felser, Ph.D., in his as-yet-untitled upcoming book about precognitive dreams and 9/11. It will be published in 2006 by Moment Point.)

Chapter 3: Lonesome Kangaroo Mama Blues

1. But not one hundred percent void of meaning, either: for one thing, maybe your intuitions are telling you that car model's a good one, since it's popular; and keeping track of how often the media reflects the details of your life could lead to oh, say, six hundred pounds of notebooks to pack up and carry next time you move. Also, see chapter 5.

2. Carl Jung (1875–1961) was a Swiss psychiatrist and colleague of Sigmund Freud, who broke away from Freudian psychoanalytic treatment of the unconscious mind as a reservoir of repressed sexual trauma that causes all neurosis. Jung's best-known work on the subject of the collective unconscious is his autobiographical *Memories, Dreams, and Reflections*, published posthumously in 1963.

Chapter 4: It's a Small-World Surprise

1. In an email sent to me on September 22, 2004, Mr. Hobby Shop elaborated, "I've known [the company owner] for about 15 years . . . I used to sell his model airplanes and worked at trade shows for him in the mid to late '80s up to the early '90s when he quit doing the models and started doing the remote stuff for the govt and power companies . . . He wanted me to move out there and go to work for him . . . still does . . . or run a training site out there. Don't know if I could handle all that. I have a standing invitation from him and so when we were out there on vacation [in 1997] we stopped without calling first and he gave the kids a tour."

Chapter 5: Random Thoughts, Media Feedback

1. Max Byrd, *Shooting the Sun* (New York: Bantam Books, 2003).

2. Richard Hamblyn, *The Invention of Clouds* (New York: Picador Press, 2001).

3. Bill Bryson, *A Short History of Nearly Everything* (New York: Broadway Books, 2003); quote is from page 263.

4. Or as Bryson puts it, "How we went from there being nothing at all to there being something, and then how a little of that something turned into us, and also what happened in between and since." It's an engrossing piece of work, to put it mildly.

5. "The Vikings" was originally released in 1958, when I was 13.

6. That is, the version of "The Puppet Masters" directed by Stuart Orme and starring Donald Sutherland.

7. Carl Zimmer, *Parasite Rex: Inside the Bizarre World of Nature's Most Dangerous Creatures* (New York: Free Press, 2001). You'll never experience food cravings in quite the same way again.

8. Which is one of the many malaproprian witticisms of Yankees great Yogi Berra, who also coined the phrase, "déjà vu all over again," which wouldn't have made a bad title for this book, come to think of it.

9. Well, okay, particularly Derek Jeter.

10. Ralph Kiner, *Baseball Forever: Reflections on 60 Years in the Game* (Chicago: Triumph Publishers, 2004).

11. Robert Parker, *Double Play* (New York: Grosset & Dunlap, 2004).

12. The complete title is *The Zen of Zim: Baseball, Beanballs, and Bosses* (New York: Thomas Dunne/St. Martin's, 2004). Don Zimmer also has a unique connection with my home town. As a member of the Pioneers, Elmira's minor-league team, he married his wife at the local field's home plate in 1951.

Chapter 6: Hugh and Me and Phone Calls Agree

1. Hugh had mentioned this idea to me before, and I'd thought it was an outstandingly horrible idea, and for that matter unattainable for a lot of reasons, zoning restrictions among them, or so one would

hope. But for Hugh, a private pilot who loved flying over the beautiful hills and valleys of the Finger Lakes, this was a dream about grand vistas as much as anything, and so I never expressed my dismay whenever he brought it up. Today the outermost end of the Bluff has been carved into a dozen or more housing sites, equally egregious, but the majority of this exquisite landmass remains in farmland and forest.

2. Loren Coleman, *Mysterious America* (New York: Paraview Press, 2001).

3. Neither I nor my ex-in-laws are related to Dr. Samuel Watkins, after whom the village of Watkins Glen is named.

4. According to Coleman's information, the teens were on their way to the 1973 "Summer Jam Festival" in Watkins Glen when they disappeared.

5. Prentice Hall was the original publisher of *Conversations with Seth*, in 1980 and 1981.

6. I had a strong negative reaction to Rogo's manuscript, and recommended against its publication. In 1980 the book was published in hardcover by the Berkley Group, New York, and reissued in subsequent paperback editions.

7. This murder took place in California, apparently involving two perpetrators. According to Coleman's email, one man was arrested and convicted of the crime but the charge was later dropped on a technicality. The homicide detective who worked the case claimed to know who the second killer was, but could never track the man down. More information on this case can be found at www.arthurengh.com/paranormalvideos.

Chapter 7: Of Marbles, Money, and Mulch

1. Stephen King, *The Girl Who Loved Tom Gordon* (New York: Scribner, 1999). Of course, Stephen King is a diehard fan of the Boston Red Sox, for whom Tom Gordon was the closing pitcher from 1996–1999.

2. *Garden Madness: The Unpruned Truth about a Blooming Passion* is its full title. It was published by Fulcrum, Golden, Colorado, in 1995.

3. Though I included only a few coincidence tales from others in this book, the following thoughts-tossed-out/imagination-results story from my son Sean is too good, and too emblematic of the point, to leave out. Besides which, I nagged him for two months to write it down for me, so I'd better use it, or else.

Sean writes: "I experienced a particularly interesting coincidence earlier this year, 2004. I am always looking around for images to use in stained glass projects, but it is difficult to find works that have just the right combination of heavy yet elegant lines that work in stained glass. I'm also a big fan of PBS's "Antiques Road Show" and in a recent episode someone brought in a few woodblock prints by Kawase Hasui, an early to mid-twentieth century artist.

"The prints were simply stunning and done in a style that would be easy to reproduce in stained glass. I was riveted. The Road Show's apprais-er said that the prints were of moderate value at the moment (about $500 each) but he expected that their value would rise in the near future because collectors were becoming more aware of Hasui due to the recent publication of a comprehensive collection of his work. I ran to the computer to find a copy of this book, which I fully intended to buy.

"It turned out that the book cost $300—way beyond my budget even with my discount as a bookstore employee and there were relatively few copies printed so the chances of finding a used copy later on were fairly slim. I resigned myself to looking through the tiny thumbnail images of Hasui's work that I could find on Ebay and other art dealer websites.

"About two weeks later I was working away at the bookstore and in an off moment I started looking through the boxes of newly received books. I should pause here to point out that I work in a branch of the store that deals mainly in cheap mysteries and bestsellers with precious few "interesting" or artsy titles. We stock a few books valued at about

$40 or $50 but never anything that sells for more than $100. We just don't carry expensive books and our ordering and shipping system is totally separate from the huge main bookstore downtown.

"Anyway, among all the boxes of $7.99 Custlers and Pattersons and other pulp titles there was a package that had been mistakenly dropped off at our location. The sender was a Publisher's West warehouse in California that our bookstore never uses—although we do deal with Publisher's West through another California warehouse—and the receiving address was a small independent bookstore on the east coast that has absolutely nothing to do with us. Our UPS delivery person is always extremely thorough and I have never seen any other packages mistakenly delivered to our location. Out of interest, I opened the box and what should be inside but a copy of the new $300 Hasui collection!

"I asked around and none of my fellow employees or managers could explain why this book had come to us. Pure mistake. Also, no one seemed to care if the book 'disappeared' or not and it seemed that it was mine for the taking due to a strange alignment of flawed bookkeeping that would have prevented anyone from knowing where the book had gone, and the fact that I was about the only person in the whole state who had any particular interest in Hasui. I kept the book for a week or so trying desperately to justify keeping it for good, but in the end I came to my senses, contacted the addressee and sent the book on its way."

Chapter 8: The Continuing Tale of the Cat on a Leash

1. The plant did change hands, but as it turned out, most workers kept their jobs.

Chapter 9: Didn't Do X, Which Leads to Y

1. As of December 17, 2004, the mail carrier is still in recovery with head and spinal injuries; according to a person close to the family, she is "moving in the right direction" but will have to undergo months, possibly years, of rehab with no guarantee of outcome.

2. "All of them," as my son Sean put it. Which is, of course, an observation of both empirical and intuitional truth, neatly combined.

3. Describing this incident, I made this last remark in an email to my cousin Mike Young, who replied: "Greasy food is indeed good for you once in a while.

"I was struck [he added] by the sentence in which you pondered what would happen if we dissected every possible instance of this sort of thing, how much time we would not have left . . . . It's something I've thought of—each and every dream we've ever had and the consequences of each one of them, that to have the realization of their interconnection roll over us in a single wave would certainly unhinge you, a peek at how time is a complete untruth, and that not only is everything spliced, but that it all happens at the same instant—and to us it looks like 'coincidence' that things are an echo of the Truth in this strange, worm-hole view we have of the night sky . . ."

Chapter 10: Lies I Apparently Didn't Tell

1. Maybe this sighting set a vulture precedent. Or at least ushered in avian coincidence. A week or so later, we watched another (or possibly the same) turkey vulture trying to land by a dead woodchuck in the pasture adjacent to Dave's house, though the inquisitive resident horses kept chasing the bird away. Not long after that, on two separate occasions, we drove past turkey vultures eating dead deer on the side of country highways. Magnificent!

2. Later that day, I wrote up this whole strange experience and emailed it off to my pal Glen Venezio, an energetic and intuitive person who understands this sort of thing quite well. When Glen replied that afternoon, he had an interesting connection to relate:

"HEY SUE, I am so sorry you were up all night, thinking about your plants. The strange thing on that score is that for the past 2 nights, and actually DURING the hours that you were awake last night, I have been sitting up watching a foreign film called "Inch'Allah Dimanche" (something like, "Thank God for Sunday" in Arabic), this beautiful story of a woman's journey out of the submissive role typical in Arab families—she is an Algerian whose husband has been working in France and finally he is able to bring her and their 3 children to live with him.

"In the story, their new upstairs neighbors are an older French couple who have a huge flower garden in the shared back yard, and have won competitions for the best garden, and there is a scene where the French woman is up all night worried that the Arab children are going to trample her flowers and ruin her chance of winning the prize again! And they do tear out a big sunflower, and the French woman screams at them about it. So that's kind of interesting, the connection!"

Interesting, and funny. I had to laugh at myself—all that worry, and what I finally get out of it is a neat coincidence!

Chapter 11: How Much Do We Know, and How Do We Know It?

1. See *Dreaming Myself, Dreaming a Town*, pages 33–35. Thad, outwardly a very conservative fellow, shocked me silly in the post office one day with the statement that not only did he remember his dreams "all the time," but that in his opinion, everybody in town should write dreams down and talk about them every morning—on the radio, if possible. "Better'n gossip," he added, succinctly enough.

2. Or more accurately, a previous version of the house appears in *Dreaming Myself, Dreaming a Town*, as a chapter note, page 118, quoting the "brighter days are ahead" fortune cookie message that was found unscathed in the ashes after everything else, including the cookie, burned up in a fire that consumed the entire house and all its other contents. The family rebuilt the house on the same spot overlooking the lake.

Chapter 12: An Odyssey of Letters

1. I found out about Walt's death from my research assistant Mary Dillman, actually, who had driven to Saratoga Springs in early

December for the express purpose of contacting Walt and other child-hood friends of Jane's and asking them for interviews. Mary told me that she left a message from her motel room with one of these friends and when the fellow called back, it turned out he'd just come from giving a talk at Walt's memorial service and had stopped off at his house before going on to the gathering at the Zeh family home! "He was very struck by the timing of my call," Mary said. Ditto and then some, I might add.

2. I do have (pre-war) letters written to him by my mother while she was attending college at the University of Michigan and he was finishing some fifth-year high school credits in Elmira. These tell more about my mother than my father, however—compelling, to be sure, but not what I was searching for just then. My parents met in 1932, when they were twelve years old, and according to my aunt Marie, my mother told her way back then that she was "going to marry Newell Mullin and have one child, a girl." Indeed!

3. Rex Warner, *The Stories of the Greeks* (London: MacGibbon & Kee, 1967).

4. Shortly after my father's death in 1983, my mother received a letter from Benny's fiancée, now in her sixties, long since married to someone else and living in the Midwest. In it she describes letters that my father wrote to her after Benny was killed, and, hoping against hope that these letters had somehow been preserved, I tried persuading my mother to write back and ask for copies. But she never quite got around to it, and by the time I took it upon myself to make the inquiry, the address was no longer extant, and my letter was returned "addressee unknown."

5. Interesting that not long after this, I came across this newly published book: *War Letters: Extraordinary Correspondence from American Wars*, edited by Andrew Carroll, published by Scribner, with a release date of May 15, 2001.

Chapter 14: The San Francisco Quake of '89

1. *Dreaming Myself, Dreaming a Town,* page 260.

2. Though tornadoes do touch down occasionally in the Finger Lakes, they aren't as frequent or destructive as their infamous Midwest cousins.

3. Harbor City is located near Los Angeles, so it's most likely not the same Joe Gallagher.

4. I describe the Elmira flood in some detail in *Speaking of Jane Roberts,* chapter 12.

About the Author

Susan M. Watkins is a former newspaper reporter, feature writer, and columnist, and the author of six books, including *Speaking of Jane Roberts* and *Conversations with Seth*. She lives in upstate New York. To contact her, please write c/o Moment Point Press, PO Box 920287, Needham, MA, 02492; or email her at smwbooks@yahoo.com.

If you enjoyed *What a Coincidence!*
we know you'll enjoy these other
titles by **Moment Point Press** . . .

Susan M. Watkins
Conversations with Seth
25th Anniversary Edition
books 1 and 2

Speaking of Jane Roberts
*Remembering the Author
of the Seth Material*

Jane Roberts
Adventures in Consciousness
Psychic Politics
The God of Jane

Kenneth Ring, Ph.D.
Lessons from the Light
*What We Can Learn from the
Near-Death Experience*

For more information about these and
all of our Moment Point titles, please visit
www.momentpoint.com